FREEDOM AND HAPPINESS

A Philosophy For All

JACK E. REINHARD

ISBN: 1461110343
ISBN-13: 9781461110347
Library of Congress Control Number: 2011906281
Createspace, North Charleston, SC

AKNOWLEDGEMENT

Life is a learning experience. Over fifteen years in the federal and local levels of government, while regulated by state government, has given me insights into how government works. In addition, over fifteen years in corporate operations helped educate me in how business works. Aside from formal education in engineering and economics, my greatest education has come from reading publications from very knowledgeable people in the business world. Reading what these people have published has developed into a strong respect and admiration for their views. Writings of Pam and Mary Ann Aden, Doug Casey, John Mauldin, Ron and Rand Paul, Jim Rogers, Richard Russel, Peter Schiff, Porter Stansberry and Martin Weiss have guided me to an intense belief in the free market and the opportunities it gives to responsible, independent individuals. I want to thank these people for contributing to my education.

TABLE OF CONTENTS

FREEDOM AND HAPPINESS
A Philosophy for All

A Road to the Joyful Success of the Free Individual

FOREWORD

The reason for writing this book is concern for my children and grand-children, as well as for the future generations in which they will live. The developed world of the United States and Europe has been led into high unemployment, low expectations, and money steadily decreasing in value. There is little confidence in governments in those countries and states within those countries. People are unhappy with govern-ments and the prospects available to them. The failure to provide clear and understandable leadership has caused much confusion and uncer-tainty. That is evidenced by wars and conflicts between groups and countries, strong conflict between political parties within and between countries, and a general lack of confidence and belief in the leadership of government. As a parent and grandparent, I want my children and grandchildren to live and grow in an environment that allows them to independently achieve their maximum capabilities. The ultimate goal of good parents and grandparents is for their children and grandchildren to live full and happy lives. Parents and grandparents can help their children and grandchildren only as much as they are able to use their resources. In the end, the fate of individuals is up to each individual and the choices he or she makes. The intent of this book is to help re-sponsible individuals to find a way to achieve happiness for themselves and for their children. This can be done in an environment in which most people desire the same goal. Nothing would please me more than to see my children and grandchildren live in a world that allowed them to achieve their maximum capabilities. The aim of this book is to help them and others to realize that future.

THE SEARCH FOR A BETTER LIFE

The people in the United States and Europe are experiencing high unemployment and lower expectations for improvement while their money buys less over time. Confidence has fallen in the governments of those countries and the states within those countries. There is a depressed outlook of people about the opportunities available to them. Confusion and uncertainty has resulted from their governments failing to provide clear and understandable leadership. Responsible people are doubtful as to what road to follow in order to be satisfied and happy. Many lack direction to their lives. This has increased conflicts between people, groups of people, organizations, religions, states, and countries. People, at the very least, need similar beliefs to reduce their individual confusion and help all to embrace a common ideal.

We need a philosophy that we can embrace to make this world a better place in which to live, no matter where we live or what our background. The various religious beliefs in this world have been the rationale for many conflicts. The various political viewpoints and their applications have also been the reason for conflicts. There must be something that all people can believe that will allow peaceful, progressive, and satisfying lives.

There will always be some people who are better at improving their situation and adapting to their environment, but the differences in progress should not cause negative relationships between them. The difference could also be because of perceived wrongs between ancestors long dead. Our direction should focus on adapting to current circumstances and satisfying current needs.

The ideal for people is to accept their differences by cooperating and coordinating with each other to help improve their lives. More militarily or economically dominant groups can help strengthen the weaker groups. Positive groups can also be examples to help weaker groups improve. In order to do this, we must find a way of thinking or philosophy that all could accept and follow.

This seems overwhelmingly difficult when you think in terms of broad, socially based philosophies and long-term feuds. If you begin the search for a great philosophy from the basis of simple, common feelings, you can develop an accepted way of thinking that benefits all.

To gain general acceptance of this philosophy, you need to gain the acceptance in people's minds. This is much like many religions or the denial of those religions. Whether you are religious or not, you must have some belief in the direction to your life. The direction to your life is determined by your belief in a life, or existence, beyond this one. For the basic level in developing a common philosophy, you can look at people's thinking to see if they believe in a higher order or afterlife.

Most people either believe that there is a possible higher order of our being or that you exist simply to expend time and effort in a human body for a finite time. Whether you believe in a higher order or not will not hinder you from desiring to live a better life. Your beliefs are only an outside influence on your progress toward improving your life. Other outside influences include who your parents are, where you were born, or the neighborhood in which you live. To make this issue simple to understand, it is easier to approach this quest as though you have no preconceived ideological belief. As we go through this thought process, we can add environmental influences and how you will react to them to achieve a better life. It is easier to build this philosophy if we limit our environmental influences by considering no affiliation other than simple existence. You can be considered to be a limited individual.

FINDING THE RIGHT DIRECTION

Even if you believe that you have only a limited existence, you must have some direction to your efforts other than to simply age and die. It makes sense that you will desire to use your time and efforts to live as easily and well as possible. It is also likely that you will seek to be free to act in your own best interests to gain the most joy or happiness during your limited time. Your efforts would logically follow a philosophy or belief of freedom of action toward your own joy, satisfaction, or happiness.

Freedom is, above all, an individual state of being that can be applied to singular tasks, actions, or thoughts. Freedom or liberty means that you are able to independently exercise or apply your time and effort without restriction to every task of life. It is essential that you are able to choose among tasks, actions, or thoughts that can help you accomplish what is in your best interests. By having the freedom or liberty to make choices in your best interest, you can attain your fondest desires. Acts that harm other people or that prevent other people from the freedom to act in their own best interests detract from the individual who performs those acts. Reprisal from others will reduce your freedom if you harm another or, without justification, restrict his or her freedom. By actions that have no negative impact or that aid others, you can improve both your own and others' freedom. By exercising your freedom, you will have the opportunity to seek the things in life that give you pleasure or happiness.

Happiness is a feeling or emotion that fills you with a positive sensation. It also makes sense that you would seek to attain positive sensations from actions you take. Independent actions can either provide you with positive feelings or can provide positive feelings to other individuals that can multiply the impact. The positive feeling or happiness is multiplied by the number of people experiencing it because they will often return those actions or feelings. Those actions that generate negative feelings, or unhappiness, are harmful to the people involved. Negative feelings, or unhappiness, violate the freedom or liberty of individuals experiencing them because those feelings are not of their choosing. The negative feeling, or unhappiness, is also multiplied by the number of people experiencing it. No person would, of his or her own free will, choose to experience negative feelings or unhappiness.

In order to seek and attain your desires, you must be free to choose when, where, and how you can act. There are many things in our world that restrict or place barriers to being able to choose the most rapid and easiest actions. The barriers or challenges to action come from both outside and within yourself. Living in a complex world makes it a constant struggle throughout your time on earth to attain and use your freedom to improve your existence. The struggle is further complicated by trying to gain your freedom without harming others and suffering losses of freedom due to punishment or reprisal. The method to improve your freedom and enjoyment is to gain and use knowledge of the world around you. Knowledge, and the use of it, is the means to gain more freedom and use that freedom to attain positive feelings or happiness. Knowledge is obtained through the experience of actions, observations, communications, and various physical reactions that would include sights, sounds, smells, tastes, and touches. People who believe in a singular, limited existence can use their knowledge to improve their own situation as well as those of others. Those finite individuals who are considered "wise" would be thought to have unique and gifted thinking processes that give them better insight into their knowledge and experience. People who best use their knowledge will likely achieve more of what they desire than those who do not.

As limited individuals will seek to use freedom and knowledge in a positive sense to improve their lives, so also will people with religious or spiritual beliefs. The limited individuals must believe that what you achieve in this life is limited to this time on earth. The difference between limited individuals and those with spiritual beliefs is that the spiritual people must consider how their actions will affect them after this physical life is ended.

For you who believe in a higher power or universal order, you will also want the freedom to pursue a more positive, enjoyable life. You believe that each person is gifted with a soul from a higher power, a God of his or her religion or belief. If there is a God or higher existence, you can only believe that this higher power would only want the simplest objectives for all souls, whether in a human or a spiritual body. When you allow that the souls may or may not be embodied, the objectives become even easier. The difference between an embodied soul and a spiritual soul is a matter of substance, with the common characteristic of time. Both experience time, but the effect of time does not change the soul's ability to experience freedom, happiness, or knowledge. Souls experience no aging, deterioration, or the effect of the change in the environment around them. Time passes as the soul seeks to fulfill its objectives. The simplest objectives of a soul would include the following:

1. **Freedom** to choose responsibly among alternatives available without harm or damage to another soul
2. **Happiness** or joyous feeling from thoughts or actions that give pleasure and do not harm or damage its soul or another's soul
3. **Knowledge** gained from the experience of the soul that will aid in choosing thoughts or actions to improve the possibility of gaining freedom and happiness

The difference between the finite individual and the soul-based individual is in the case of the "wise" soul-based person who may carry forward some knowledge gained previously. Whether you believe in reincarnation or that "wise" people are simply gifted thinkers is whatever you are free to believe. The most sensible life objectives of each person or soul are as outlined above.

"Freedom is the oxygen of the soul."

Moshe Dayan

Freedom to choose life alternatives is as applicable to a soul-based being as it is to a finite being. They will both seek to gain freedom and will both seek to use that freedom to improve their existence. Some religious or soul-based individuals may believe that they must endure pain and/or suffering during their physical life to be rewarded in the afterlife. Those individuals will seek to gain more freedom and improve their time in this life, hoping their hardships were meant for a limited time. As soul-based people, they can believe a just God may limit their pain or suffering. As physical beings, we can never know what our God will consider enough punishment. Even considering the worst case of punishment, you would expect that all would seek to gain and use their freedom to select the best life alternatives.

Satisfaction, happiness, or joy is not limited by whether or not a soul is in a body. It is hard to imagine a being that has never experienced positive feelings about something in the time of existence. Having experienced a single instance would likely cause that being to desire more positive happenings. The desire to gain more happiness is a universal objective of all beings, whether or not soul based.

"The basic thing is that everyone wants happiness, no one wants suffering. And happiness mainly comes from our own attitude, rather than from external factors. If your own mental attitude is correct, even if you remain in a hostile atmosphere, you feel happy."

H.H. The Dalai Lama

THE PHILOSOPHY OF FREEDOM AND HAPPINESS

Without a difference in your belief or spiritual makeup, you will desire freedom and liberty. Freedom is a basic right and state of being that allows you to act and develop to the maximum of ability or talent. Your religious and spiritual thinking must revere and be thankful for the freedom and abilities with which you were born. It is your responsibility to make the most of those gifts. Whether or not you were born into a religious environment, you owe it to your parents and yourself to make the most of the freedom and abilities that came with your birth. The limits of your environments will place some restrictions on you, but your efforts and actions determine your level of freedom.

It is only logical that you will also desire to be happy. Happiness is not a right, but is a feeling, sensation, or emotion that is a positive result of mental or physical actions. It is a goal or objective that can happen in a free atmosphere. The free atmosphere is not necessary, but most certainly aids the attainment of happiness. Without freedom, the ability to gain happiness is, without a doubt, much harder. As freedom is an individual state of being, so it is necessary for you to search and attain happiness with as little restriction as possible.

The combination of freedom and happiness is a basic description of goals that you can follow. There is nothing negative about you desiring freedom and happiness. There is no harm to anyone for you pursuing freedom and happiness when it is done at no one else's expense. As a way of life or philosophy, it is positive and will help those who choose to follow it. It is up to you to find the best way to apply this philosophy. Knowledge gained and applied will be the key to success for you.

The key to improving your freedom and increasing the opportunity for happiness is by increasing your knowledge. Knowledge to improve your environment in order to gain freedom and attain happiness is not limited to whether or not you are soul based. How you are able to gain knowledge varies, depending upon the environment that you experience. A soul-based individual will have beliefs and guidance that comes from one's religion. A limited individual will have to gain knowledge from a world similar to the world that a soul-based individual experiences. Whether religious beliefs are helpful or harmful depends on how open you are to learning from the environment. A religion that reinforces freedom and knowledge may improve your ability to learn, but one that limits freedom and knowledge could make it more difficult for you to learn from the environment.

Knowledge to improve your freedom and happiness will be gained through various types of environments that you experience. Aside from the religious beliefs that you may subscribe to, there are several environments that can help or hinder gaining more freedom to seek happiness. Those environments are the following:

1. Religious/spiritual
2. Political/governmental
3. Legal/judicial
4. Market/business
5. Social
6. Mental/emotional

RELIGIOUS/SPIRITUAL ENVIRONMENT

It is not conceivable that a higher power would want to restrict the freedom of its followers. Even limited individuals would believe that freedom is a right that transcends religious beliefs. Those who believe in a higher power believe that there are rules or guidance from which to live. They use those rules to conform to the people around them to avoid causing any harm or discomfort to them. Those limited individuals who do not believe in a higher power may also wish to avoid causing harm or discomfort to others, so that they can avoid reprisal. All individuals who seek freedom would agree that they must act responsibly. By avoiding possible reprisal from others, you are able to pursue freedom. You can be sure that you do not cause others to wish to make you unhappy or dissatisfied. It is, therefore, best for you to avoid undue discomfort or harm by others that will reduce your freedom to pursue happiness.

Whether you are Christian or not, you can use those core tenets to lead a life without strife caused by others. Even those who do not believe in a higher power will act responsibly to avoid strife by either following or not violating these core guiding principles. The following ten core tenets are known as **God's commandments**:

1. Thou shall have no other Gods before me. (People should only have one God or higher power that they believe in.)
2. Thou shall not make unto thee any graven image. (People should not worship or believe in any image other than the one of their God.)
3. Thou shall not take the name of the Lord thy God in vain. (People should not call out or use the name of their God without reason to call to him.)
4. Remember the Sabbath day to keep it holy. (People should devote the day that their religion observes to worship their God.)

5. Honor thy father and thy mother. (People should give respect to their father and mother.)
6. Thou shall not kill. (People should not cause another person's death.)
7. Thou shall not commit adultery. (People should be true to the one they marry and should not desire to harm others in their relationships.)
8. Thou shall not steal. (People should not take from others what does not belong to them.)
9. Thou shall not bear false witness against thy neighbor. (People should not give false information about others.)
10. Thou shall not covet. (People should not envy what is not their own property.)

A nonreligious person will not observe the first four commandments, though they may not disobey them. That person may not clearly observe the first three, but will not violate them because they do not believe in God or any god. For commandment number four, a nonreligious person could follow a practice of peaceful aid to fellow citizens one day per week. Though this is not the same as going to a place of worship, this may be considered keeping holy the Sabbath by other individuals. At worst, you would only live a nonreligious life that was considerate and cooperative. In terms of giving you the chance for freedom of choice and access to knowledge to gain happiness, you are not prevented from freedom and happiness.

The last six commandments deal with how you treat others. Judgment on the severity of harm to another would determine whether a person would be considered by themselves or their fellow persons to have violated a commandment. When you interact with another, it is difficult to know what if any harm was done. You can easily determine whether or not another is killed, lied about, or committed adultery. It is more difficult to determine if a person has dishonored their parents or coveted fellow individuals or their things. You could simplify the determination by requiring the loss of something valuable in terms of measurable time, money, or goods, but how could you know the value of feelings or emotions? That decision would be complicated if you did not know the people's backgrounds enough to understand what may hurt their feelings or upset them emotionally. Perhaps the best choice in dealing with others is to reserve judgment on what you say and focus on positive actions and communications. To promote freedom and happiness, you must not consciously take either away from another in your dealings with others.

A point to consider in terms of freedom and happiness is that people who live "good" lives must be doing it from their own free will. People who, on a day-to-day basis, act only according to the small, detailed dictates of a religion to which they belong are not being truthful to themselves or to those around them. These people will not be able to consistently act freely and will not find happiness or be able to honestly increase others' happiness. It is difficult to find happy hypocrites or happy friends of hypocrites.

When considering the religious/spiritual environment, you have to look at the chance of how it helps in gaining freedom and happiness. Freedom and happiness will not be gained if you do not operate in a peaceful environment. Following the commandments will assure that you will have a better chance for a peaceful life. You do not have to be religious to follow the commandments, yet you must choose how to act. In this world, you have to be free to choose your beliefs and how you practice them. If there are restrictions placed on religious/spiritual choice, you lose an opportunity for freedom. Without religious/spiritual freedom of choice, the peaceful atmosphere that allows a chance for happiness is sharply reduced. While a free religious/spiritual environment can provide the peace, government can provide the order needed to gain happiness.

POLITICAL/GOVERNMENTAL ENVIRONMENT

Government is a system of order that provides a means to serve groups of people with common functions. Government exists at several levels—local, town or city, county, state, national, and international. Local government sometimes acts within a town or city and would be like a school district, hospital district, neighborhood association, town-house association, condominium association, or professional association. Each level of government focuses on serving a larger number of people as it grows from the local size to the international size.

Basing the functions of various sizes of governments, the preamble to the U.S. Constitution gives six functions of government:

1. **To form a more perfect union:** The government will be fair across different jurisdictional boundaries, helping keep the functions of each working together.

2. **To establish justice:** The government's responsibility is to protect those who do obey the law and punish those who do not.

3. **To insure domestic tranquility:** In order that all may lead a tranquil and quiet life, according to their own conscience, in a godlike and dignified manner.

4. **To provide for the common defense:** All life is held as sacred, with the protection of innocent life at the base of capital punishment. The government is to provide protection from external and/or criminal threats.

5. **To promote the general welfare:** Civil rulers are servants for the general good. All classes of citizens are to be represented equally by any laws the government may pass. The government may not provide or aid special interest groups above others. It is to promote, not provide, for the people.

6. **To secure the blessings of liberty:** As stated in the Declaration of Independence, blessings are endowed upon men by their creator, not a privilege granted by government. These blessings include life, liberty, and property. Government cannot provide these, only secure them.

Many believe that the God of our forefathers inspired the creation of the Constitution of the United States. Although not perfect, the U.S. Constitution has lasted for over two hundred years and has been the blueprint for liberty in many nations around the globe.

The size of government is usually proportional to the geographic or population size that it manages or controls. Legal systems within civilized countries define the legal boundaries to minimize conflicts between governments of different sizes. Conflicts are not completely avoided, so compromises between two sizes of government are sometimes required. An example might be the U.S. law against killing another person, while the punishment for homicide is different in states. This type of compromise allows different applications in the operations of a government to reflect more localized standards. Local compromises work similarly between state and town jurisdictions in utility regulation, drug enforcement and regulation, and other services that are provided or regulated by different levels of government.

In theory, the first function of government of forming a more perfect union would allocate power fairly across the different levels of government. In current practice, there is close cooperation between local and state governments. Over the last three decades, the power of the United States federal government has grown as its spending has grown unheeded by budgetary controls. This was helped by a politically cooperative Federal Reserve. The result of this growth in power caused a growth in dependence on the federal government, and this, in turn, caused state and local governments to lose control and the ability to function responsibly. While many social benefits increased from the federal level, so has the debt and dependence of citizens increased. The state and local governments are levels at which citizens have the most influence, yet have lost the power and ability to best serve their citizens. As U.S.

citizens' knowledge increased of the country's debt growth and loss of personal freedom, so did dissatisfaction with the federal government.

Politics are applications of philosophies that help determine who, what, when, where, and how a government is operated. As government either regulates or provides services for citizens, politics is the philosophy that drives those government functions. If a government is to successfully serve its citizens, it must have a philosophy to promote freedom of choice to allow those citizens to seek their happiness. In order to allow the existence of freedom of choice, there must also be a free society that allows and supports communication between and among individuals. Without freedom to communicate, there cannot be adequate knowledge for people to freely make choices that are in their best interest. With freedom of communication and freedom of choice, you will know that you had the opportunity to participate in the government that serves you. Though government rules, regulations, and laws may or may not be your preference, you may choose whether or not to support the government's direction and experience the results of your choice.

Some philosophies believe that government should be focused on property and how it should be protected and used. The most valuable property of an individual is freedom. It is that property that allows each of us to seek happiness. It is that freedom that allows us to gain knowledge that helps us find the things in life that give us happiness.

However a government serves an area or citizen group, they are going to try to satisfy those they serve. A government that does not satisfy and improve the well-being of its citizens will not be able to continue with the same philosophy for long. If the government is attempting to serve the citizens within its jurisdiction, the ultimate objective should be their happiness. If happiness is the government's objective, it is necessary for it to allow and promote individual freedom. With each person free to choose what will make him or her happy, there is the best chance for a government's citizens to be happy. It is each government's obligation to assure that it can promote individual freedom while preventing harm to any citizen. This has long been a difficult task that requires a type of government to balance order with individual satisfaction.

Order, as in the case of religious freedom, must be maintained to allow people the freedom of choice so that they can attain happiness. People need rules and regulations to promote actions that do not cause measureable harm to others. Without restraints on harmful individual or group actions, freedom of choice can be prevented or limited. The challenge facing a government is in defining what is harmful to a person or group when creating rules or regulations. Building upon the freedom and happiness philosophy leads to these defining characteristics of what should be considered as harm:

1. **Harm prevented:** Measureable harm to others must be prevented by government rules and regulations, while promoting and supporting freedom and the opportunity to attain happiness. At the same time, there must not be harm to a person or group to promote another individual or group.

2. **Harm must involve others:** The harm must be to someone other than the individuals themselves. If people make a choice that may harm them, it is their decision and should not be subject to another's selection. For example: If a person chooses to eat, drink, or act in a manner that is recognized as being harmful (drinking alcohol, smoking, a high-fat diet), that person should not be prevented by the government or other uninvolved entity from that choice.

3. **Harm must be measureable:** The harm must be measureable in real terms. If the harm cannot be measured in a manner that is acceptable to most others, then it cannot be justly mitigated. A damage or injury that cannot be easily verified by sight or measureable quantity cannot be justly prevented by a rule or regulation. For example, an injury to someone's feelings is not measureable if a person or group of people cannot know the intent that an action had on the victim or the intent in which the action was delivered (slogans and posters during political contests come to mind).

Of the six functions of government, five are related to maintaining order, and the sixth is applicable to maintaining freedom. With order in place, freedom can be attained, and happiness can be gained. The functions of the various levels of government are meant to be equal and beneficial to all of the citizens of each governmental body. It is up to each person to attain whatever level of benefit that he can from his efforts. At the same time, it is fair that the level of benefits that a government provides is paid for by the receivers in proportion to the benefit level provided.

Government and governmental services are not free. People and resources are used in order to provide such things as roads, water, sewer, energy, communications, and police and fire protection. Some of these services are provided by a division of a level of government, or they are regulated by that level of government. Whether government services are provided directly by the government or through regulated services, there are expenses involved. Those expenses are paid for through taxes or service charges. In order to maintain freedom and the ability to seek happiness, the taxes and charges must not harm some to benefit others.

Using the freedom and happiness philosophy, fair and just taxes and charges can be accomplished by the following:

1. Assuring that taxes and charges to an individual, group, company, or organization do not unjustly prevent freedom of choice
2. Assuring that taxes and service charges are directly proportional to the level of benefit to the individual, group, company, or organization
3. Assuring that taxes and service charges do not provide benefits to individuals, groups, companies, or organizations beyond what they either earn or for which they pay

With freedom allowed and promoted in an orderly government that assures fair and just taxes and charges for services, the citizens of a government will have an equal ability to attain happiness.

In recent years, the expansion of governments has resulted in government providing many functions and responsibilities that are the responsibility of the individual citizen. There are certain functions and responsibilities that logically and economically are best handled by government. General protection (police, military, and firefighting) and transportation (streets, highways) are two areas that appear to be best served by government. There are several services that are, and can be, served by either government, private, or corporate operations, such as water supply, sewerage disposal, education, electricity generation and distribution, natural gas production and distribution, and air and land transportation services. Services and responsibilities that go beyond the grey areas above (feeding, clothing, income, and housing) take away the freedom (and dignity) of the receivers and reduce the freedom and happiness of those who are forced to pay for or provide them.

Much of the expansion of government benefits has occurred at the national level or because of standards set there. In the United States, congressional and regulatory actions that expanded the benefits of government have been funded either by deficit spending, currency creation by the Federal Reserve, or by "unfunded mandates." Unfunded mandates are rules and regulations that are passed down to state and local governments with funding left up to those governments through taxes or service charges. With an economy that is growing, state and local governments have little challenge in meeting those expenses. With a shrinking or declining economy, there is a growing burden on states and local governments to fund additional expenses. Unlike the federal or national governments, state and local governments cannot print currency (create money) to increase expenses beyond balancing their budgets.

All services, whether they are provided by government or not, have the goal of providing a value to the receivers of those services. The value of those services depends upon satisfying the citizens that they serve. The most obvious measure of the effectiveness of a service is the perceived return of the customers that they serve. The return is the perceived value, and the investment is the cost of the service or responsibility. The perceived value is what the receivers of the service feel they have gained from the service. It may also be what they think it would cost them (time, money, stress, relief) if they provided the service for themselves or their family. The investment is the cost of the service in capital, time, or other expense.

Private or corporate investments are evaluated in a free market environment that will determine the value of the service by survival of the service. For government-provided services, the value is not as apparent as survival. The real determinant with a government service is whether the cost of it is considered too high a price to pay for it. This will show up in a number of ways, such as utilization of the service (for competing services such as utilities), complaints to elected officials (police, fire, military, streets, highways, drainage, or transit services), or poor customer/citizen relations with government representatives in all services. All services that are provided by government operations are subject to the judgment of those they serve. The success in pleasing their citizens is dependent on how free the citizens are in choosing to use them. It is also dependent on the opportunity the citizens have to pursue happiness in using those services. With most services and responsibilities, there is the opportunity to please or satisfy the receivers because they chose to receive them of their own free will.

The highly expanded form of government attempts to provide services and benefits beyond what the majority of free, independent individuals want. The expanded services are often created by a government to provide more security and reduce the risk of individuals having to provide for themselves. Services such as protective, transportation, or utility services are willingly supported by and available to the majority of taxpaying citizens. Government services and benefits like food, clothing, housing, and income are only freely supported by the receivers of the services. In fact, they must be supported by taxing all working citizens who would not choose to support those services if they were free to choose. Freedom and happiness is taken from the majority of taxpaying government citizens to provide expanded services to some citizens. This is done in return for security, some satisfaction, less freedom, and less dignity or pride to a small number of citizens receiving those expanded services. Under the expanded form of government, citizens do not have the freedom of choice to benefit from taking risks that may cause a loss or failure.

A free and just government following the freedom and happiness philosophy promotes and supports freedom of choice and gives all citizens the equal opportunity to attain happiness. Citizens who use services that are either regulated or provided by government will have an equal opportunity to improve their conditions. All citizens will have the same level of government support and the same level of cost for government. All citizens will have the same opportunity to attain happiness through government supplied or regulated services.

With a government that promotes freedom of choice through its rules and regulations, while promoting order, the following can be achieved:

1. You will have the sole responsibility for your improvement without government interference. You would be able to operate in an orderly environment that gives you the opportunity for happiness.
2. You will have an equal opportunity to improve your chance for happiness through use of government regulated or operated services. At the same time, all citizens would have the same treatment by regulated or provided government services.
3. Those citizens who have been successful at attaining happiness will have the freedom of choice as to how they will maintain their situation. All citizens will contribute equally to those services that they receive from their government in the same proportion to their benefit.

Providing order is a purpose of government, whether through providing or regulating services. The government functions that are the focus of political and public influence are subject to the citizens' opinions in determining their success. The freedom and happiness philosophy will help in promoting freedom of choice and satisfying their citizens' desires.

LEGAL/JUDICIAL ENVIRONMENT

The legal environment of the government is that function most focused on providing protection, order, and justice. The first ten amendments to the United States Constitution set the basis for the legal system within the United States.

===Preamble===

Congress of the United States begun and held at the City of New York, on Wednesday the fourth of March, one thousand seven hundred and eighty nine.

THE Conventions of a number of the States, having at the time of their adopting the Constitution, expressed a desire, in order to prevent misconstruction or abuse of its powers, that further declaratory and restrictive clauses should be added: And as extending the ground of public confidence in the Government, will worst ensure the beneficent starts of its institution.

RESOLVED by the Senate and House of Representatives of the United States of America, in Congress assembled, two thirds of both Houses concurring, that the following Articles be proposed to the Legislatures of the several States, as amendments to the Constitution of the United States, all, or any of which Articles, when ratified by three fourths of the said Legislatures, to be valid to all intents and purposes, as part of the said Constitution; viz.

ARTICLES in addition to, and Amendment of the Constitution of the United States of America, proposed by Congress, and ratified by the Legislatures of the several States, pursuant to the fifth Article of the original Constitution.

===Amendments===

First Amendment to the United States Constitution

Congress shall make no law respecting an establishment of religion, or prohibiting the free exercise thereof; or abridging the freedom of speech, or of the press; or the right of the people peaceably to assemble, and to petition the Government for a redress of grievances.

Second Amendment to the United States Constitution

A well regulated Militia, being necessary to the security of a free State, the right of the People to keep and bear Arms, shall not be infringed.

Third Amendment to the United States Constitution

No Soldier shall, in time of peace be quartered in any house, without the consent of the Owner, nor in time of war, but in a manner to be prescribed by law.

Fourth Amendment to the United States Constitution

The right of the people to be secure in their persons, houses, papers, and effects, against unreasonable searches and seizures, shall not be violated, and no Warrants shall issue, but upon probable cause, supported by Oath or affirmation, and particularly describing the place to be searched, and the persons or things to be seized.

Fifth Amendment to the United States Constitution

No person shall be held to answer for any capital, or otherwise infamous crime, unless on a presentment or indictment of a Grand Jury, except in cases arising in the land or naval forces, or in the Militia, when in actual service in time of War or public danger; nor shall any person be subject for the same offence to be twice put in jeopardy of life or limb; nor shall be compelled in any criminal case to be a witness against himself, nor be deprived of life, liberty, or property, without due process of law; nor shall private property be taken for public use, without just compensation.

Sixth Amendment to the United States Constitution

In all criminal prosecutions, the accused shall enjoy the right to a speedy and public trial, by an impartial jury of the State and district where in the crime shall have been committed, which district shall have been previously ascertained by law, and to be informed of the nature and cause of the accusation; to be confronted with the witnesses against him; to have compulsory process for obtaining witnesses in his favor, and to have the Assistance of Counsel for his defense.

Seventh Amendment to the United States Constitution

In suits at common law, where the value in controversy shall exceed twenty dollars, the right of trial by jury shall be preserved, and no fact tried by a jury, shall be otherwise re-examined in any court of the United States, than according to the rules of the common law.

Eighth Amendment to the United States Constitution

Excessive bail shall not be required, nor excessive fines imposed, nor cruel and unusual punishments inflicted.

Ninth Amendment to the United States Constitution

Protection of rights not specifically enumerated in the Bill of Rights.

The enumeration in the Constitution, of certain rights, shall not be construed to deny or disparage others retained by the people.

Tenth Amendment to the United States Constitution

Powers of States and people.

The powers not delegated to the United States by the Constitution, nor prohibited by it to the States, are reserved to the States respectively, or to the people.

The Preamble to the Constitution was written to protect citizens from unfair government. At the national level in the United States, the expansion of power of the federal government has been interpreted more broadly over the years to gradually give it more power. Less power and ability was given to state and local governments while, at the same time, greater responsibility was thrust upon them. Citizens have the most influence on local and state governments, and those levels of government have now lost their ability to provide services that best address local needs. Although the courts provide order and all courts follow the preamble, major decisions have gone to higher courts, which have given greater power and authority to the national government. The result of high-level court decisions has gradually given more power to the federal government to assure that the majority of U.S. citizens must follow the same rules and regulations as small groups of citizens.

Though the legal environment is contained within the government, it focuses on laws and regulations that can be determined in courts of law. The legal environment goes deeper in determining actions than the policy and procedures that make up the broad function of government. Laws are set by various levels of government to help maintain order, and maintaining order prevents individuals and groups from harming others. While preventing harm to others, freedom and liberty must be preserved. As in the case of freedom of choice in government, individuals also have the freedom to choose how they comply with laws, while avoiding harm to others. Government enforces laws that apply to how individuals and groups act toward the laws created by some levels of government. There are also laws that apply to how damage claims between individuals or groups are to be judged. As in the case of differences in laws and regulations between levels of government and different countries, different philosophies are applied. In looking at different laws and regulations, you can only try to choose what makes the most sense in trying to support freedom and maximize the opportunity for happiness.

As laws develop and are interpreted to apply the freedom and happiness philosophy, we must keep in mind an ideal. Considering laws and regulations that will allow and support freedom, prevent harm to others, and allow development of happiness, the following seem to make the most sense:

1. Harm must be measureable in some generally accepted manner. Measurable would mean the following:

    a. A loss of life
    b. A visible physical injury or damage
    c. A cost, loss, or penalty of a dollar amount, or
    d. Creates a situation/condition that increases the risk of one of the above

2. Harm must be to another person or group. Any harm that does not detract from the freedom of or cause harm to another should not be considered a crime or law violation. Examples include drug users or compulsive eaters who damage their health without harming others unless they take from others to support their habits.

3. Claims for damage or injury must be allowed only if the risk for losing the claim is the cost of all legal work. The claim must be measureable harm and enforceable by law, as in the following examples:

   a. An unsuccessful damage lawsuit that claims a loss in property value would cause the person filing that suit to pay the legal fees of the defendant in addition to his or her own, or

   b. A criminal case against an entity, if unsuccessful, would subject the government making the case to paying the defendant's legal bills.

An individual or group must have the freedom of choice to be able to make a criminal or civil claim against another individual or group. As important as it is to maintain freedom of choice, it is also important to avoid harm to others. Poor or untrue claims that may harm others must be avoided in a just society. In order to prevent unwarranted claims, there must be a risk of loss for the individual or group making the claim. The saying that "a person is innocent until proven guilty" is a true statement that supports freedom and liberty of the individual.

A result of the application of the philosophy of freedom and happiness applied to the legal system would be that criminal and civil cases may move through the legal system more rapidly. Looking at some examples of criminal cases gives these situations:

1. Criminal case where defendant is guilty and knows it. The legal authorities would not charge a person unless

they were sure of being right, so they would not delay in making a charge after gaining enough proof. The defendant would not want to delay reaching a verdict or paying his sentence because he would not want to generate legal fees.

2. Criminal case where defendant is innocent and knows it. The legal authorities would not make a charge if there were a risk of it costing their department the costs of the defendant's legal fees. A defendant who knows that he is innocent will get the best attorney because the attorney does not have to worry about getting paid.

3. Criminal case where the prosecuting enforcement agency is unsure of defendant's guilt. The agency will spend only enough effort to either prove the defendant's guilt as necessary, or it will drop its efforts.

Applying the philosophy of freedom and happiness to civil cases would work similarly. The lawyer for the entity making a claim would act much like the prosecuting attorney in criminal cases. There must be a risk associated with any tort action. An unsuccessful tort action should result in a loss of freedom or finances in a free and fair court system.

Using the freedom and happiness philosophy in the legal environment can bring about the following results:

1. A truly fair system that will provide freedom from unwarranted criminal or civil claims against individual citizens

2. Lower numbers of criminal and civil cases in the courts for offenses that had no identifiable victim or risk of measureable harm

3. Lower numbers of imprisoned people awaiting trial or imprisoned for offenses that had no identifiable victim or risk of measureable harm

4. More rapid movement through the courts, if for verifiable identified offenses that had a readily identifiable victim and/or risk of measureable harm
5. Lower insurance rates to cover civil and criminal liabilities for only reality-based claims with strong supporting proof
6. Lower legal costs in criminal and civil cases with as much risk for an accuser as it is for a defendant

Though the ideas expressed in this document may differ from some of the current laws in place in the United States or some states, the intent of the Bill of Rights is still maintained. The differences are in the expanded idea of government. It attempts to transfer benefits to individuals who are judged to be more deserving, regardless of freedom or equality considerations. The bottom line for a legal system that supports freedom and gives opportunity for happiness may seem in conflict with the current system. What must be considered is that justice must be the maintained so that freedom can exist and happiness can be attained. Justice will assure that freedom is not taken or restricted from those who deserve it and will be taken from those who do not. Happiness will not be taken without legal reason and can be attained by just settlement of realistic claims.

BUSINESS/MARKET ENVIRONMENT

The legal/judicial and government environments are two areas that were given emphasis by the founding fathers of the United States. Most people have heard of the "Boston Tea Party," which was a protest against the British taxing and attempted control of the tea market. When the United States set up its laws and its government, freedom of the individual and freedom of the business markets was intended and expected. When the United States freed itself from Great Britain, it became a country of free individuals with free markets.

"In a capitalist society, all human relationships are voluntary. Men are free to cooperate or not, to deal with one another or not, as their own individual judgments, convictions and interests dictate."

Ayn Rand, Capitalism, The Unknown Ideal

The philosophy of freedom and happiness should feel at home in the business or market environment. Most people have heard about capitalism and the concept of the free market in which the value of a good or object is determined by what people or companies will pay for it. The free market is you, me, and all the people who work to earn a living and make the choices that are in our best interest. Within a free market, the price of a good is determined by supply (S) and demand (D) curves. On a supply curve, supply level is determined by how much people will pay for a given supply level of a good. On a demand curve, the price of a good determines how much of that good that will be purchased. Where the two curves, drawn on the same chart, intersect, they will determine the normal price and volume of a given good available on the free market (see chart below). The normal free market price and volume of something is the fair and just price.

The free market is the way markets will work under normal circumstances. When short-term circumstances cause the volume and value of an asset or good to vary, there will be a correction back to the free market value and volume. Short-term circumstances are caused by local events (earthquakes, hurricanes, tornadoes, hail storms), changes in goods' availability, factory shut downs, or regulatory changes (rules and regulation changes by a local, state, or federal authority). The short-term circumstances can cause variations in the supply of or demand for a good from the free market. These circumstances do not eliminate the existence of a free market or the capitalist economic system. Distortions of the market will make their corrections back to the free market level over time. The greater the distortion or variance, the longer that it will take to correct it. The capitalist, free market, economic system is the natural way the business/market system will always work.

THE FOLLOWING FIGURE SHOWS THE SUPPLY AND DEMAND CURVES IN A FREE MARKET. CHANGES IN DEMAND CAUSED BY GOVERNMENTAL OR ENVIRONMENTAL ACTIONS IN THE FREE MARKET (D1 AND D2), CAUSE CHANGES IN THE PRICE (P) AND QUANTITY (Q) OF A GOOD.

P

D1   D2   S

P2

P1

Q1 Q2   Q

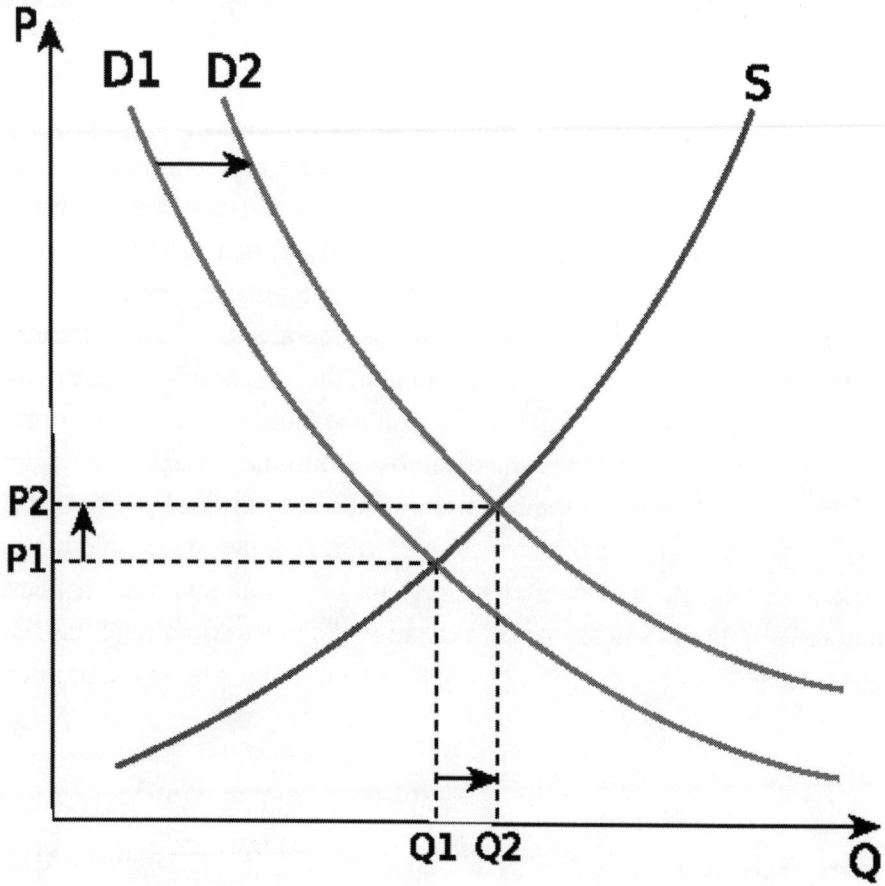

Supply and Demand Curves

P= PRICE
Q = QUANTITY OR VOLUME

In the case of any object of value, including cost of labor or people's pay, the free market determines how much it is worth and how much the market will use or buy. Unfortunately the market may be free, but the way it values something is not always the way people desire it to be. The market is distorted by participants who use misleading communications to push purchasers into making decisions to gain short-term advantages. The market also can be distorted by regulations that attempt to make desirable results that do not agree with a free, normal market.

It has been common among many governments of the industrial countries in the world to attempt to manage the free market. They use tactics that distort the market by attempting to manage interest rates, regulations on hiring practices, regulations on loan management, and regulations on trading of securities. These attempts to create artificial, short-term aberrations of the capitalist, free-market system are likely to fail. History and failed governments help to verify this. Market manipulation by governments has caused the failure not only of the distorted economic systems but has also the governments that supported them.

The United States and members of the European Union governments have been most active in managing the financial and business markets by using unbacked (fiat) currency or money. These governments release data that support their financial tactics. Often, the data do not appear to represent what their citizens experience. In the United States, there is a Web site ShadowStats.com that provides alternative statistics on unemployment, inflation, and gross domestic product (GDP). In the United States, financial data that you see on TV or read in the news may not seem to make sense or follow supply-demand economics. Using the best information available in pursuit of freedom and happiness, you must do what is best for you and your family.

Any attempt to prevent the natural, free exchange of goods and services must fight the natural tendency for you to enjoy freedom and to gain the joy and happiness that is natural for you. Economic systems that attempt to alter the natural freedoms of individuals and restrict them from the pursuit of happiness will not survive.

SOCIAL ENVIRONMENT

The social environment is challenging because of its complexity. Ideally, you can react to the world in an objective manner that will be most beneficial to you and to those for whom you are responsible. In reality, there are pressures from others that can influence how you interact with others. Peer pressure is a recognized influence on behavior. In recent times, there are now legislative or regulatory restrictions (examples: discrimination, human resource, and harassment laws and regulations) that attempt to impose government control of social interactions. With other people or groups, or even government, attempts exist to influence how a free individual should communicate and act.

If you are to be free and have the opportunity to gain happiness, you must be free to make decisions as to how to interact and with whom you interact. Restrictions should be limited to concerns with harm to others and beliefs based on factual history. The factual history that influences your actions can include the environment (social, financial, family, or religious) that you have experienced or your mental state. All considered, social interactions by you on a given issue should be choices based on reality. It should not be trying to please the perceptions of others.

Rotary International has a test that can be used to determine how we interact with others. It is called "The Four-Way Test" for the things we think, say, or do and it reads as follows:

1. **Is it the TRUTH?**
2. **Is it FAIR to all concerned?**
3. **Will it build GOOD WILL and BETTER FRIENDSHIPS?**
4. **Will it be BENEFICIAL to all concerned?**

If the above test were used in individual interactions, the complexity of "modern" society and regulation of personal interactions would be much improved. If each communication were tested for truth, there would be no need for rules or regulations to determine if there was real damage done by the communication. If the communication was true, how could the subject of the communication blame someone other than themselves? If the interaction (communication or action) was fair to all concerned, how could there be harm done to anyone? If the communication or action built good will and better friendships, there should not be a problem for anyone outside of those involved. The involved parties would certainly feel better about the other people concerned. If the communication or action is beneficial to all concerned, then all will be better off than before the action. If individuals follow the Rotary Four-Way Test, the social environment will work for all.

One of the issues that cause more conflict than necessary is that individuals and groups of individuals tend to desire to let past inequities influence present actions. This is most obvious in issues involving religious, racial, tribal/national, family, or language histories that some feel should be the basis of present communications or actions. Histories cannot be the basis of unjustly punishing or rewarding individuals or groups in the present. No doubt, if individuals had materially harmed another or committed a crime in the past, they are liable in the present. There is no good reason that an individual or group should be punished or rewarded for religion, race, tribe/nation, and family or language history. With social interaction, the past should be left in the past and the present used for decisions on what we say or do.

Social interaction has changed as the technology of communication has evolved to a high level. Although the means of communicating has changed, the content and quality of communication can follow the same principles. Over the last fifty or sixty years, the ability to use various communication technologies has strayed from the Rotary Test. What was once the principle of reporting news changed to providing news and information with differing viewpoints. Is the news you read in the paper or see on TV the truth, or is it only true about some of the details that are given to you (leaving out details that do not support the writer's or speaker's view)? Is what you read or see on TV or in advertisements fair to all concerned? Is it only fair to those who the writer, speaker, or artist wants to promote (consider political advertising here)? Will what you read, see on TV, or in advertisements build good will and better friendships? Will it focus on only the negative aspects of the subject in order to promote another subject? Will it be beneficial to all concerned, or will it only be beneficial to the person or issue being promoted (while ignoring the harm done to others involved in the issue)? With today's technology, there are so many ways to use deceptive communications to promote actions that are not in the free individual's best interests.

The social environment at the present time is challenging because so much of it is outside of your control. You can apply a Rotary Test to all social interactions to avoid harm and conflict. The Rotary Test, like the Ten Commandments, the Constitution Preamble, and supply and demand economics, can help bring freedom and the opportunity for happiness. If the philosophy of freedom and happiness is followed, social interactions will be based on the present reality. There will be no restrictions, limitations, or harm based upon the past. Using the above guidelines will help your social interactions free you to develop a happy social environment.

MENTAL/EMOTIONAL ENVIRONMENT

The mental and emotional environment is mostly an internal environment. It is the thought and emotional pattern that develops over time from our history or traits inherited from our ancestors (and former souls if you believe in reincarnation). You will have as much control over your mental and emotional abilities as you choose. You must choose to be a free thinker and free to experience the world around you if you want to seek freedom. Other individuals will seek to limit or restrict how you think. Early in life, those individuals may be parents, grandparents, brothers, sisters, or aunts and uncles. You could hope that you had older family members who encouraged you to think freely. Whether they did or did not, it is likely that the human spirit within you would seek to choose to gain as much freedom as possible. You could also hope that the older family members helped you to learn those actions that help develop stable thinking and emotional patterns. With the help of family and application of the God-given desire for freedom in your environment, you will eventually gain a level of freedom. If you have not become a free thinker before you leave your family, as an adult you can become a seeker of freedom and happiness.

As is the case with the related social environment, the mental/emotional environment is complex. Interactions with family while growing up, relations with others in various environments, and communications from various media all influence your mental/emotional internal environment. The complex outer world must be handled to gain a sufficient level of freedom to apply the knowledge to reach a fulfilling level of happiness. You can gain a level of control over the outer world by reaching a comfortable balance between mental and emotional abilities.

"The aim of life is to live, and to live means to be aware, joyously, drunkenly, serenely, divinely aware.

Henry Miller (1891_1980)

The challenge to reaching a balance between metal and emotional abilities is as great today as it has ever been. Many young people grow up with parents who do not have as much time to spend with their children as needed. Children are raised by substitute guardians who have little or no concern for them. Information is gained from media that desires to sell goods to the parents or the children and is not concerned with educational or helpful content. During preadult years, much information is gained from media or from other young people. The Internet has provided the means to acquire knowledge and information. Although the quantity of information available on the Internet is enormous, there is no filter to determine the quality or truthfulness of the content. There is the danger of becoming a creature of the media (TV, radio, Internet, or cell phone) with no thought or emotion of your own.

The technological advancement in media sources has increased our challenge to assess mentally and emotionally reliable information. Entities that have much political or financial power can manipulate the various media to promote ideas, products, or people to provide convincing information that may not be true. These entities can use sight, sound, pictures, or scenes that are studio contrived rather than scenes from reality. In highly developed industrial countries, there is information available that gives other viewpoints and may contain real-istic information. In a busy world, it is difficult for you to avail yourself of the vast array of information sources. With limited time, you need to develop an independent means of dealing with information to which you are exposed.

You cannot be totally in control of a logical thought pattern, and you cannot be totally responsive to feelings or emotions. As an individual seeking your own freedom, you will need to free your mind and heart to be truly representative of who you are. As in the case of the social environment, you must use the past for knowledge while avoiding carrying negative views or feelings to the present. The Rotary Test can be used on memories as well as on information that you are exposed to in the present.

1. **Is it the TRUTH?**
2. **Is it FAIR to all concerned?**
3. **Will it build GOOD WILL and BETTER FRIEND-SHIPS?**
4. **Will it be BENEFICIAL to all concerned?**

When you have an experience in your day-to-day living, you can test it just like you may test what you would hear or say. Is what you experienced real and true? Did you personally witness it, or was it on film? If televised, was it live or filmed? Can you personally verify what you heard or saw? Can a highly reputable source verify what you heard or saw? Are all your questions related to the experience answered? Does the reality and truth of the experience support or reduce your freedom of thought?

Was what you experienced fair to all concerned? Was your experience just and impartial? Was the experience of all others concerned fair, just, and impartial? Was anyone harmed unjustly? Did anyone gain unjustly from the experience? Was freedom of thought and expression supported by the experience in a fair and just manner for all concerned?

Does what you experienced build good will and better friendships? Does what you experience help those involved to improve your relationships? Does what you hear or see work better with others? Does it improve some people's feelings while harming others' relationships? Are all related to the experience improved in a positive way?

Does the experience benefit all who are concerned? Does the action from what you see, hear, or experience help all or only some of those involved? Does the experience harm some to benefit others?

You must take into account the testing of your experiences along with the positive values gained as you approach your life's independence and freedom. Part of aging and experiencing life is learning from your environment and the people in it. The above tests can also help to gain the most positive knowledge and experiences from your past and current environments.

If you want to free your thinking to attain freedom and gain happiness, you must be oriented positively, both mentally and emotionally. In today's complex social and communication environment, it will be challenging to gain the freedom necessary to seek happiness. Applying a testing standard will gain and maintain free thinking and positively oriented knowledge for a happy emotional and mental state.

HOW YOU CAN GAIN FREEDOM AND HAPPINESS

The world that we live in is composed of many complex environments, viewed in a segregated time and space manner. Unfortunately for each person, we each experience some or all the different environments at the same time. It can seem overwhelming to try to deal with all that we can be faced with at the same time. In addressing the same previously described environments, we have to find a way to deal with them in a simple, easy manner that does not take us too far off the desired path. The path is to gradually free yourself and your thinking so that you can gain adequate knowledge to reach a happier, more joyous existence.

The best method for choosing and following a path is to first choose where you want to go. In general, we want to be free to think and act in the best way to gain more knowledge and to choose what will make us happy. Over time, we will choose various activities, people, and thinking that give us joy. As we grow in knowledge and experience, these activities, people, and thinking may also change. We may stray from the path, but we can get back on, if we keep in mind where we are going.

Now, some people will start to get confused about their direction because knowledge and experience change what they value that makes them happy. There is nothing wrong with this. Nobody ever said that life was simple and easy.

And we're all owed joy
sooner or later
The trick's to remember whenever
it was, or to see it coming.

Carol Ann Duffy (1955)
British poet

As Ms. Duffy says, we may experience joy and happiness in memory, or we may know what we want in the future. It may mean that, over time, we go back to things from which we found happiness in the past. It is overwhelmingly important that we do gain and retain enough of our freedom, so that we can make the choices necessary to make us happy.

If we are to recognize what made us happy in the past or what we want in the future, it is important that we do not forget our objective. The objective is to gain and retain personal liberty or freedom, so that we can choose to do what will make us happy. This is what must be kept in mind as we follow our path through the various environments in our lives.

COPING WITH THE RELIGIOUS/SPIRITUAL ENVIRONMENT

There are many religious philosophies that you can adapt or follow. With the current types of media (written, radio, television, film, Internet, or electronic), you can learn about many religious beliefs or philosophies. The cultures of some areas may limit what is allowed to be available to you. In any area or culture, there is always the option of not following a religion or even being opposed to any religion. Whether you are religious or even antireligion, the philosophy of freedom and happiness can still be followed.

The previously mentioned limited or finite individuals can take either of two directions in dealing with the religious environment. This depends largely on how socially active they are. Individuals who are introverts and tend to avoid social occasions have an easier time in managing the religious environment. Limited introverts can avoid going to church and to religion-related social events. They avoid any challenging social religious conversations and causing any negative actions by others because of differences in religious belief. They can follow the last six of what are called God's commandments, while not disobeying the first four. The limited individual can be a good person who does no harm to another or causes any actions from others that could restrict their freedom and opportunity for happiness. The limited individual can improve opportunities for happiness by helping others to improve their happiness in some way.

A limited individual who is more socially active has a challenge to gaining support for increasing and maintaining freedom. Religions and religious social events are a major part of some areas' social life. Limited individuals can avoid going to religious services because it has become acceptable in today's society to miss religious services. Religion-related social events pose a difficult challenge. It is even more challenging if the individuals avoid being truthful. They can tell inquisitive people, "I believe in being a good person and have not chosen a religion." A statement along those lines may not satisfy the strongest religious followers, but it will not offend them and bring about reprisals. If they follow the last six commandments and the Rotary Test, they will not offend anyone by their actions. As in the case of the more introverted limited individual, the more extroverted limited individual can improve opportunities for happiness by helping others to improve their happiness in some way.

Whether an introverted or extroverted limited individual, there should not be an attempt to use strong efforts to convert others to a certain view of religion. A person or group that forces belief in a religion or limits a soul's direction takes a basic freedom away. This reduction in personal freedom will, at the very least, cause negative reactions from many people. It will, without a doubt, reduce the ability of individuals to have the freedom to choose the best path to happiness.

The person who lives in an area where there are religious dictates must deal with religious beliefs of one or a number of them. Whether limited to only one or few religious choices, you can nevertheless follow God's commandments. It does not matter what the highest level religious leader is called: what matters is how people act with others and in their world. The Ten Commandments are guidance in how people should act, regardless of their religion or the name of the figurehead of it. It is up to you to avoid harm to others that will bring reprisals that limit freedom. Religions that would be interpreted to harm others are not positive for you and your path to freedom and happiness. Individuals or groups that require only one religion take away the freedom to choose your best path to happiness. If you live in a restrictive or limiting religious atmosphere, you must try to follow the Ten Commandments and avoid harm to others (as the commandments would expect). If you decide that your religious environment is too limiting or restrictive, you should move to a location more suited to your beliefs.

Some individuals are fortunate enough to live in areas where there is a choice as to what religion to follow or whether to not follow a religion. These individuals live in areas where there is freedom to choose their religion and how they practice it. People in areas where freedom of religious choice exists have the advantage of being able to follow the Ten Commandments in any religious environment. The advantage of living in an area with an option to choose how to satisfy your spiritual needs gives you a step on the path to freedom. You may have some influence from family and community in choosing a religion. However, as you age and develop toward independence, you will be able to choose what satisfies your freedom and happiness objective. There will be choices to make in your personal development to take you further down the path to more freedom and happiness.

"I call that mind free which jealously guards its intellectual rights and powers, which calls no man master, which does not content itself with passive or hereditary faith, which opens itself to light whensoever it may come, which receives new truth as an angel from heaven."

William Ellery Channing (1780-1842)

Where you can choose your spiritual direction, there are many choices. The Internet and various other reference sources provide much information about different religious and spiritual philosophies. The differences in various faiths are in the details or practices of the particular religion in question. No religion that consciously and purposefully allows you to do harm to another supports individual freedom or aids in the pursuit of happiness. An individual who follows such a religion should avoid any procedures or dictates of that religion that would cause harm to others. In the same religious situation, you can nevertheless follow the Ten Commandments to satisfy your religious responsibilities. Following the guidance of the Ten Commandments does not mean that you must be involved in a religion. As in the case of the limited individual, you do not have to be a member of a religion but could simply follow the commandments.

Membership in a religious organization or church usually entails a certain level of related social activity. In some areas, there may be pressure to join a religion to fit into the social scene. Religious freedom does not mean that you must be a member or follower of a religion or socially pressured to belong. As William Channing so addressed it, the idea is to gain spiritual freedom. The idea is to choose a spiritual direction, which may or may not include a particular religion. In choosing the most comfortable and enjoyable spiritual path, you can do the following:

1. Examine the various religions of which you are aware and the spiritual beliefs or ideas that give you the most freedom to learn and develop your life to be happy.
2. Of those beliefs and ideas, determine which will make you and the people you most care about happy.
3. Test those chosen beliefs and ideas to see if they are in accord with the Ten Commandments.
4. If those beliefs and ideas are in accord with the Ten Commandments, then see if those beliefs and ideas closely fit a particular religion or faith.
5. You can do either of two things.

    a. You can choose the religion that most closely matches your ideal and only follow the spiritual beliefs and ideas that make you most free and happy.
        Or,
    b. You can independently follow those beliefs and ideas that most make you both free and happy.

The exercise of spiritual freedom will give you a basis for living so that you can gain freedom in all the environments in which you live. With a base of spiritual freedom, you can achieve freedom that can lead to increased happiness.

COPING WITH THE POLITICAL/GOVERNMENT ENVIRONMENT

The government is another environment with which you must also cope to gain freedom and seek happiness. We are all served by several levels of government. The politics of government is the philosophy that each government follows to provide us services. The functions of a government have been defined by the founders of the United States. Government is supposed to serve each individual and provide the following:

1. **A more perfect union:** fair across different jurisdictional boundaries, helping to keep the functions of each working together

2. **Justice:** by protecting those who do obey the law and punishing those who do not

3. **Insure domestic tranquility:** that all may lead a tranquil and quiet life, according to their own conscience, in a godlike and dignified manner

4. **The common defense:** as all life is held as sacred, with the protection of innocent life at the base of capital punishment—the government is to provide protection from external and/or criminal threats.

5. **Promote the general welfare:** by providing service for the general good: all classes of citizens are to be represented equally by any laws the government may pass—the government may not provide or aid special interest groups above others: it is to promote, not provide, for the people.

6. **Secure the blessings of liberty:** as stated in the Declaration of Independence, blessings are endowed upon men by their creator, not a privilege granted by government: these blessings include life, liberty, and property; government cannot provide these, only secure them.

In addition, we have the Bill of Rights, the first ten amendments to the Constitution of the United States. These amendments were made to protect individuals' civil rights.

The above is all that you can expect from your government, at any level. You can expect the government to protect your rights and allow the freedom to avail yourself of opportunities in your environment. You must act as though it is up to you to provide for your own good and that of your family. Adults, of course, must provide for their children until they are old enough to provide for themselves. Adults may, when necessary and within their ability, provide for a spouse, parents, and brothers or sisters. It is up to you whether or not to provide for anyone outside of your immediate family. It is also each independent individual's responsibility to pay for government services that he or she uses. It is, above all, the responsibility of government to give you the freedom to be able to provide for yourself and seek to attain a happy existence. The above six functions of government give the opportunity for you to live free and happy.

There is no doubt that the government, during its early days, had much different ideas and ideals. They were different from what the current citizens in many governments are experiencing. The early leaders in what became the United States were in the upper levels of educated society. They had taken great risks to have come to this country and took great risks to gain freedom from England. It cost some their lives, their fortunes, and their families. It is obvious that they felt that freedom was worth all that they had, even their lives. They gave the people of the United States a gift that was worth all that any can imagine. It is our responsibility to try to live up to the principles with which we were gifted. This only provides more support for personal efforts to gain freedom and use it to gain happiness.

Now, we must get to the point and see what we, as individuals, can do to cope with the current levels of government. In general, each person should not act in ways that would harm others. Orderly government can give an individual the atmosphere to improve and develop. Supporting an orderly government can help each person. Conflicts with levels of government and with other citizens will hamper development and can cause reprisals, including imprisonment or fines. So, basically, you can help yourself by avoiding conflicts with government or other individuals. At the same time, you must remember that there are times when you must act in the best interest of freedom and the right to seek happiness. This thinking is what the founders of the United States must have gone through.

One of the conditions that the people in many developing countries must face is the desire for people to gain happiness. In some areas and in some times, the desire for some individuals to gain happiness overcomes the desire for freedom. In those places and times, the desire of individuals for better homes, food, clothing, professional medical care, and income overcomes the desire for freedom. In that political environment, they steer their government to take from the most successful to provide for their housing, eating, clothing, health care, and income. It is normal for an individual to want to do better and be happier. In the type of government that the founders of the United States envisioned, some individuals' freedoms and abilities were not to be unwillingly reduced or taken away to improve the lives of others.

"That all men are by nature equally free and independent, and have certain inherent rights, of which, when they enter into a state of society, they cannot by any compact deprive or divest their posterity; namely, the enjoyment of life and liberty, with the means of acquiring and possessing property, and pursuing and obtaining happiness and safety."

Virginia Bill of Rights, 1776—George Mason (1725—1792)

As our forefathers realized, the idea is for all to have equal rights and not require that we gain our rights and freedoms by taking them unjustly from someone else. In supporting order, you cannot take freedom, rights, and property from others to provide free benefits for those who have not earned them. This places a strong responsibility on government to use the resources derived from taxes and payment for services in a prudent manner. By being sensible with funds from those with taxable income or profits from services revenue assures that all individuals' freedoms are invested fairly. Though many would like to help those less fortunate than themselves, it is the government's responsibility to use our resources wisely. It is our responsibility to support government actions that provide benefits to others in proportion to what they have contributed to society. Is it fair to provide housing benefits to a healthy adult who has never earned an income equal to the costs of housing that person? Is it fair to provide basic necessities of life (food, clothing, and health care) to those who have never earned enough to even provide them the basic necessities? Most people do not mind providing short-term help to individuals who normally earn a living by providing services or goods to others. At the same time, most people would not support giving up a share of their earnings to help others who make little or no effort to earn a living for themselves. You will need to consider if it is a fair trade off to give up some of your freedom and happiness to help others to be happier.

Individuals face some of the following examples of local, state, or national government actions:

- Local housing authorities that provide houses or apartments and housing maintenance for individuals and families
- Medical care at emergency clinics for all who come in
- Lunch programs for individuals and children
- Unemployment benefits for those without jobs
- Payments to individuals and families for food, clothing, and shelter

As a free individual, you will not mind paying for services provided to another in proportion to the benefit that you gained from those services. The challenge for individuals who want to gain the most freedom to pursue happiness is, how much of your freedom and income do you give up to help others (charity)? This challenge is made even more difficult when you consider assistance to others outside of a local area or even outside your country. In the case of aid or assistance beyond what is considered the local area, you must seriously consider what that aid or assistance does for yourself or your local area. Will helping someone elsewhere improve your freedom and ability to gain happiness in your local area?

As a free individual, you can judge how well any level of government functions by looking at the budgets. A balance between revenues or income and expenses should exist more often than not. It is not tragic to spend more than received for a government in a particular "down" year, but that should be an unusual occasion. Many government operations, city, county, and state have mandates to have balanced budgets. As a freedom-seeking person, you should expect that the government that serves you has a balanced budget. It should be the object of your government to have a balanced budget. More prudently, it should build a surplus during "up" years to allow for a balanced budget during economic downturns. At the government level serving you, you should expect that it will not fund projects or expenses outside of your jurisdiction without first balancing the local budget. A balanced budget at your level of government will assure that you are not giving up your freedoms or rights to another government or level of government. It is difficult for you to be free if your respective government gives up some of its freedoms or rights to another government or level of government. It will be more difficult to be free to seek happiness, if your government limits your freedom by increasing costs beyond the income it has available. You should choose to live in an area where your government is able to manage its finances without imposing future liabilities on its citizens.

The larger a government is in population and area, the greater the possibility of it using funds outside the local area or even outside the country. With the size of government increasing, so do the responsibilities of that government. Though responsibilities may increase with size, the relations outside of the local government jurisdiction do not increase proportionately. The first responsibility of any government is to provide services to its citizens. Actions and responsibilities of your government outside of its jurisdiction should be to improve or protect the freedom and ability to gain happiness of its citizens. As in the case of balancing a budget within a government, there must be a balancing of efforts between benefitting the government's citizens and helping another government or group of people. Again, the question should be, does helping someone outside the local area help the freedom and ability to gain happiness of the citizen in the local area?

There are many examples of actions that individuals of "wealthy" countries face, if you look at the international scene:

- Funds and aid to foreign countries
- Military bases in foreign countries
- Military aid to foreign countries
- Trade agreements with foreign countries
- Loans to foreign countries
- Diplomatic offices/embassies and missions in foreign countries

For countries and states involved in international relations, there has become an accepted practice of allowing and encouraging overall expenditures that are greater than the resources gained. When total expenses exceed income of a state or country, this will cause inflation within that state or country. There may be inflation within a country as it takes more of that country's currency to buy natural and real resources with currency that gradually decreases in value. There may not be a loss of freedom and ability to gain happiness in comparison to other countries, if all other international participants in trade inflate their currencies at the same rate. However, a country with a larger trade deficit and larger average budget deficit will lose freedom and happiness to a country with a trade surplus and a balanced internal budget. As an example of an extreme situation, a double deficit country will decrease its freedom and ability to gain happiness, while a double surplus country will increase its freedom and ability to gain happiness.

We have a good example of governments as described above. The United States is an example of a double deficit country, while China is an example of a double surplus country. Over the last decade, unbiased judges have seen the citizens in China gain freedom and the ability to gain happiness while the citizens of the United States have lost the same. It is fortunate for the citizens of the United States that their level of freedom and opportunity for happiness was much greater than their Chinese counterparts at the beginning of this trend. Individuals living in a "wealthy" country like the United States, with only an infinitely small influence, must exert what influence they can to improve the freedom and happiness of themselves and their fellow citizens. As citizens of a country that continues to exhibit double deficits over a number of years, we must do what is in our power to support improvement in the functions of our government.

Discussion of some of the many aspects of government has been limited at this point to illustrate the influence of government on our lives. In a civilized society, government plays a major role in the level of freedom that you can attain and the ability to gain a level of happiness. The complexity of government makes it difficult for you to understand how to best function to improve your personal environment. It is best to try to provide the simplest path for you to best cope with the complicated government environment that serves us as citizens. The following will help to give some guidance on what you can do to seek freedom and improve your happiness in the government environment:

1. **Determine how government most impacts your time and money:** Examine where government most influences your life and the future you desire. Think about your job or the job that you are seeking (work/school or job/school hours make up approximately one-third of your

weekday time). Think about where you spend your funds in terms of categories like taxes, energy, food, family, nonenergy utilities, payments on loans, leisure activities, and maintenance of assets like autos, homes, furniture). In general, think about where you spend the bulk of your waking time and funds. Determine in which areas most of your personal/individual resources are used.

2. **Determine how you can best improve or reduce government's influence:** Start with the government influenced or controlled activity in which you invest the most time and/or money. Determine the activity that you can influence now (within the year) or within the future (greater than a year). Think about what level of government activity is involved in the activity. Think about who or what entity in that government action has the most influence on your invested time and money. Think about the issues that most influence that entity in their decisions. Think about how you, an individual, can convey what is needed to the government entity to influence them to improve your freedom and happiness in their decisions. Think about strategies to reduce government influence or action on those resources where you invest the most time and money.

3. **Act, as best you can to gain your freedom:** When you identify how you can influence a government body or person in their decisions, take action in the most efficient effective manner that you can. This may be a trial and error activity as a person often has to get involved to learn as well as do. As an individual, keep in mind that singular action may not be effective, but there will be others who will feel the same. Over time, if you are right, the numbers supporting your thinking will grow, and you can eventually reach your objective. Finally, the best way that you can improve a government body's influence on your life is to

alter your life to reduce that body's influence to gain more freedom and better improve your chance for happiness.

Government has grown as an influence on people's lives, as has the size of government. Individuals have greater influence at the smallest levels of government. You can have much more influence at small, local levels of government because in democracies there are going to be a lower number of people voting in local elections covering smaller numbers of voters. Beyond the ability to vote, individuals have the opportunity to invest time and money in political campaigns. In addition, once candidates are in office, they are still able to be communicated with via telephone, Internet, and mail. With lower numbers of voters in local elections, government officials realize that individual and active citizens have some influence. Whether the government official is elected, appointed, or normally hired, a citizen has influence on the thinking and decisions of that official due to the democratic process.

The larger in size and population the government body, the lower the influence of an individual. That should not deter your actions, because it is possible that you can still have an influence, if you can increase your level of activity to match the size of government body involved. As mentioned with regard to size and locality of government, you must weigh your own freedom and ability to gain happiness against the efforts needed for a cause. By applying the methods mentioned above, you can increase your freedom in the government environment and gain improved freedom in your life.

COPING WITH THE LEGAL/JUDICIAL ENVIRONMENT

An orderly environment is a key to seeking the freedom needed to gain happiness. An orderly environment can only be secured with a legal/judicial system that supports freedom and liberty of the individual.

"Law is order, and good law is good order."

Aristotle (384_322 BC)

Most people do not wish to experience reprisal from those entities that enforce just laws and regulations. There are laws and regulations at all levels of government that provide guidance for individuals to potentially experience peace and freedom. You can gain happiness through your own efforts by avoiding harm to others and following most of the laws and regulations within your level of government.

The same laws and regulations apply to judgment of issues in civil actions to gain reimbursement for damages to others. Whether the legal question is a civil or criminal situation, laws and regulations guide the outcome. Those laws and regulations are supported by the courts in their application to individuals and groups. The courts are not required to settle disputes or differences because applicable laws and regulations can be used as references between individuals or groups. Settlements can be reached between opposing sides by individuals and groups with or without attorneys or courts.

Something to keep in mind in legal questions or issues is the difference between criminal actions (requiring settling with a government entity) and civil actions (settlement between individuals and/or groups). A criminal action requires that the person or group charged must be proven guilty beyond a reasonable doubt through a court, while a civil action may only require a ruling by judge, jury, or compromise between opposing parties to reach a conclusion.

The criminal and regulatory laws vary in most areas. It is relatively easy to become knowledgeable of those laws or regulations that are most stringently enforced locally. It is your responsibility to learn what to do to avoid criminal action that may reduce your freedom. Although it should be easy to avoid criminal charges in an area, activities in some local areas will increase observation by enforcing authorities. In those areas, it will require you to learn the local political and societal views or actions that could cause undue and, sometimes, unjust actions by authorities. Some examples of situations that would warrant reducing visible actions would be leading active militant Muslim demonstrations in a strongly Christian community or smoking marijuana with friends in the front yard in a beer- and liquor-drinking community. Although both actions may be technically legal, they could cause enough negative feelings in the community that some may (anonymously) file complaints with local authorities. It would be the local authority's responsibility to investigate and thus could hamper your freedom severely, if done often enough, even if no criminal charges develop. You could choose to either find a more compatible, agreeable place to live or to avoid public actions that may generate negative feelings from the neighbors.

There are criminal and regulatory laws and regulations that generate much more loss of time and cost of enforcement than necessary while only restricting the actions of adult individuals. Some of the laws and regulations that waste time and funds in their enforcement include the following:

- **Environmental regulations:** laws that inhibit or restrict use of an individual's or group's property beyond what measureable impact it may have on others
- **Drug enforcement:** laws that criminalize the personal use or sale to others for personal use of drugs by consenting adult individuals
- **Sex-related enforcement:** laws that inhibit or prohibit performance or sale of services or goods between consenting adult individuals

Time and funds are expended on regulating the above issues by all levels of government. There are differences in enforcement in different areas that display the difference in the amount of freedom that is allowed or tolerated. If the freedom of the individual is considered, many of the laws related to the above issues would be eliminated. Reasons to regulate and control the above issues are as follows:

1. To protect individuals who have not reached a level of knowledge to make choices for themselves
2. To protect an individual or group of individuals from measurably harming others

In other words, regulations should promote individual freedom and common sense to thus prevent measurable harm to others. Victimless crime laws miss the obvious free choice direction of allowing adults to make their own decisions. Instead, they tax all citizens to pay for protection from such perceived harm. Unfortunately common sense and free choice are suppressed in areas and countries where time and money is spent to regulate individual adult behavior.

How can you cope with regulation that wastes resources to suppress freedom of choice? As mentioned in the section on coping with government, you can support office holders and candidates for political office who champion freedom of choice. Aside from voting, you can do any or all of the following:

1. Contribute time and/or money to political campaigns of free choice candidates.
2. Identify groups who are politically active in the freedom of choice issues that you feel most strongly about and contribute time and/or money to those groups.
3. Become involved in a political party that has the most freedom of choice viewpoint and invest time and/or money in changing their direction to more closely resemble your own.

4. Use electronic and conventional media methods to communi-
    cate support for more freedom of choice. You can contact gov-
    ernment officeholders, electronic and printed media operations,
    and groups or organizations of related thinking.

Efforts by one person are not usually successful with singular, iso-
lated attempts. If you believe in the cause that you want to promote,
you will need to be persistent to gain any level of success. As mentioned
before, you must weigh your own freedom and ability to gain happiness
against the efforts needed for a cause.

Coping with the civil section of the legal system in an area that allows individuals or groups to file claims against other individuals or
groups places risks on the freedom of people with property and assets.
Of course, the old saying "ain't got nothing, got nothing to lose" applies
to those with minimal property or assets. For those who have, through
work, payments, and savings, accumulated property, there is risk of loss
to someone who has nothing to lose. In many areas, particularly in
the United States, it is relatively easy for one person to file a civil suit
against another. This situation is the result of laws and courts that do
not require the same level of proof of claim as in criminal court pro-
ceedings. In addition, the legal system sometimes protects those filing
a claim from counterclaims by defendants. The once strongly enforced
principle of innocent until proven guilty is not applied the same in civil
suits. People and businesses must carry insurance and expend funds to
buy insurance against the possibility of being sued. An honest, reliable,
dependable, and safety-minded individual may not really need to have
insurance for protection. All people, however, pay for it when they buy
services from that individual. This is because the legal system in many
areas allows barely justified claims that potential defendants must cover
with insurance to cover legal expenses, even if there is little or no settlement. Because plaintiffs do not have to conclusively prove their claim,
defendants are often faced with the option of spending more legal fees
to defend themselves or buying peace with a settlement less than potential legal costs. There is also the risk of a jury paying a claim against

someone they view as "rich" to someone they view as deserving, regardless of conclusive proof of damage. With the possibility of an individual with little or no net worth filing a lawsuit, the possibility of a successful countersuit is reduced even further.

If you feel that the civil legal environment has little impact on your life, look at the prices that you must pay for medical services, medicine, engineering design, engineered structures, and any technical equipment. Most items that surround us have "overhead" built into them to pay for risk-related costs and the legal expertise needed to protect businesses from those costs. It is not just a matter of nominal wage rates that makes other countries produce goods and services costs below the industrialized countries. Part of the higher-cost standard of living that the industrialized countries have is the risk from legal actions that those industrialized countries must build into their business costs. Though nonindustrialized countries' costs will rise as their legal systems evolve, the industrialized countries must allow more risk in legal actions to improve their competitiveness.

The above civil legal environment is a challenge for you to live freely, without fear of having to protect your property. The obvious solution is to not own anything to have to protect. There are a number of other options:

1. Assure that enough insurance is carried to cover the possibility of a lawsuit.
2. Live and dress to avoid appearance of one who is "rich."
3. Set up legal barriers and protections to make lawsuits difficult or highly expensive.
4. Obtain residence in an area that makes lawsuits difficult or highly expensive.
5. Support public officials and judicial officials who favor tort reform.

For the majority of people who are not high-income types, all of the options above may not be reasonable. Freedom-seeking individuals will find it necessary to pick the best methods for protecting their property in progressing to a happy life.

In coping with the entire legal environment, you must keep in mind the ultimate goal is the freedom to seek happiness. The legal environment in which you live can be most helpful if used to your advantage, while pitfalls are avoided that will harm progress. By following the above methods of coping with the local legal/judicial environment, you can gain and maintain your freedom and have the best opportunity to achieve happiness.

COPING WITH THE BUSINESS/MARKET ENVIRONMENT

People in many areas of the world are faced with much doubt as to whether or not the free market works. In particular, the economic crisis that started in 2007 and continues to the present makes one wonder whether the free market has a function in the business world. Many governments are attempting to expend great sums of money to try to revive the level of business activity that was enjoyed up to 2007. The funds that the national governments are spending are, in many cases, more than their current revenues can match. With reduced tax revenues, this means that lower levels of government are also spending more than they receive in taxes and fees. National governments are creating money by printing greater sums of currency beyond the amount equal to income from taxes and fees. This reduces the value of the currency and creates debts that will be paid by the citizens of those governments in future years. This deficit spending and increased level of indebtedness is one of the reasons that the current financial crisis exists. Another reason is the tremendous amount of risk that the central banks of countries allowed the large financial organizations to undertake. This happened because the central banks, through several minor financial crises, supported the large financial businesses' survival. This willingness of central banks to bail out large financial institutes, of course, allowed them to believe that they would not be allowed to fail. They could therefore take more risk. In addition, the central bank and the legislative branches of government encouraged weaker controls on financial decisions that large businesses were making. Like children who are allowed to have as much candy as they desire, the financial institutions overconsumed until they became ill. In turn, the economies of the countries in which they existed became ill.

Now, the countries and their central banks are attempting to rationalize their past errors by communicating to their citizens that traditional economics of supply and demand must be further controlled by government. The reality is that financial and business problems are the result of government and central bank decisions. A further reality is that in the long run the basic economics of supply and demand will work in spite of government and central bank actions. Government and central banks can only distort the financial environment in the short term, and the free market will eventually dominate.

How can individuals or businesses survive, gain freedom, and increase happiness in a market that is being distorted by their national government and their central bank? The strategy that you must adapt should begin with the idea that you can best work with your local environment. The national business environment, unless you are involved in business at the national level, must be reduced in impact as much as possible. All this is easier said than done because the world has gotten smaller with so many interconnected activities and much stronger communications through the media. So many decisions by individuals and businesses are the result of perceptions that are influenced by various media. They include television, radio, telephonic communications, Internet information, written or transmitted advertisements, books, magazines, and data and/or information transmissions. Today's small world makes it all the more difficult to gain more freedom and increase the opportunity for happiness in the business/market environment.

"Chiefly the mold of a man's fortune is in his own hands."

And

"If a man looks sharply and attentively, he shall see Fortune; for though she is blind, she is not invisible."

The Lord Chancellor of England, Francis Bacon (1561_1626)

As mentioned previously, you must try to minimize your exposure to the negative aspects of the national markets and trends. This begins with looking at where and how you provide for yourself. If you are not already knowledgeable of the following, you should answer these questions:

1. Where do you earn the bulk of your living? Consider your largest source of income. Consider other sources of income, like hobby income, retirement payments, interest income, dividend income, and investment income.

2. What major trends influence the financial health of your major income source? Do you work in an industry or field that is growing or contracting? Is your employer or your company able to compete effectively in the market? What business organization is successful in your business or industry?

3. Can you find another source of income that will reduce your dependence on your present main source? Can you transfer to a more successful organization in your industry? Can you improve your company to better compete in your industry? Can you improve your other sources of income to reduce your dependence on your present main income source?

4. Are your basic skills and abilities able to be educated or trained to allow you to move to a position that is more secure? Do you have skills and abilities that you could sell or market in your area to provide your own income source?

5. If your skills and abilities can be used in a more secure and stable job, can you find a way to adjust your standard of living for a happier situation?

6. When you are working, can you put money aside until you have saved at least three months of take-home pay? This will reduce the stress resulting from a sudden loss of income. It also gives you funds to use for retraining or to use in seeking a new job. Think of this as an investment in happiness, even if it is never used.

The best outcome for the above line of questioning would be to discover that the industry in which you work is growing and stable, while your company is a top-rated provider of goods or services. In the event that you do not work for such a business, keep in mind that companies and industries are subject to trends and business decisions that value survival of the business over loyalty. Although it may be more rewarding to stay in a higher-paying job or career in a risky environment, it is up to you as to how much risk would be acceptable to be happy. As you seek freedom and the opportunity for happiness, you have to make decisions that are best for yourself and your dependents. Even in the best circumstances, you should look for the best opportunity to improve your freedom and opportunity for happiness.

As mentioned previously, the local environment is easier in which to work. You will know the local business environment, the people involved in it, the local market for people in your business, and the local prospects for growth or contraction. In short, knowledge provides security by allowing plans and actions with a better chance for success. Success in business is proportional to the amount of risk an individual or business is able to handle successfully. You can reduce the risk that you or your business must face by learning and knowing the local business environment.

Aside from your means of earning a living, there are many ways that the markets and the economy affect you. In the present time, the immense spending on national government programs and the resulting budget deficits will mean the following:

- Taxes will increase to reduce debt, and/or
- The purchasing power of national currencies will be reduced to allow wage rates to increase enough to pay for the spending at present tax levels.

For you, this means that either you will have less to spend from your present income, or you will need higher income to pay more for goods and services. Either of the choices will reduce freedom and the opportunity for happiness by causing you to work harder for the same improvements in your life. This points you to a number of strategies needed to help increase your freedom and opportunity for happiness.

The obvious choice with a restricted take-home income is reduced spending on nonessential items for a comfortable, acceptable standard of living. A lot of people have items or activities that are not "must have" or "required" expenses in their life. You should ask the following questions to reduce expenses:

1. Where and on what is most of the time and money spent from your earnings in the last month?
2. Which of these items do not improve freedom and happiness? If they do not, can they either be reduced or eliminated?
3. If those items remaining contribute to freedom and happiness, how much can they be reduced without reducing freedom and happiness proportionately?
4. Can all these items be reduced enough to generate savings for your emergency funds?

You must consider the above within the context of family obligations. Spouses and children must be considered to gain support of decisions. Children, unable to live and work independently, will need to cooperate to follow the direction of their parents.

Another strategy to consider beyond your main source of income is on the secondary income side. A second job with the same tax and possibly additional related spending may not be a good alternative. Secondary income can be beneficial to increasing your, or your family, take-home income. Some of the considerations that you or your family should consider are the following:

1. If an activity brings in additional revenue, how much of this revenue requires reporting to tax authorities? Some activities do not require record keeping, because they are all both buying and selling cash transactions between people. With those

transactions, there is just as likely a taxable gain as a taxable loss. Trading collectibles among amateur collectors comes to mind.

2. Of activities carried on outside a job where tax records are required, how much of your expenses are able to be counted against all your taxable income? In other words, use every tax write-off possible. If you are regularly operating in a taxable activity, you should either use a good tax software program or tax accountant to maximize all tax reductions. An example of this would be a weekend farmer who is a welder during the week.

3. Are you knowledgeable in activities that do not require public records that generate requirements for detailed record keeping? An example would be one who is knowledgeable and active in swap meets and knows the value of all types of collectibles. A swap meet regular will need to report a major sale of a rare collectible to someone who will likely report the purchase cost. It would be a waste of time to report all the small transactions in which there were minimal profits or losses.

The above considerations help generate additional income and hopefully generate more expense records to reduce taxes. It would not be prudent of an author to suggest that people evade taxes. However, by reducing the time and effort of record keeping for tax purposes and by diversifying income, you can increase your freedom and gain an opportunity for happiness.

The previous discussion in coping with the business or market environment addressed how you earn your living, how you could reduce spending, and how you could either find supplements to your income or deductions against income. If you consider living elsewhere, you can reduce the drain on income by moving to a location with lower taxes. National taxes are the same no matter where you live. There are many taxes aside from the national taxes. In the United States, there are state income taxes in all but five states, there are sales taxes of one kind or another in all locations (states, counties, and cities/towns), there are property taxes in all locations, and there are income taxes in some cities. If you are choosing to move for your job or for retirement, it pays to look at the level of taxes that you would pay in alternative locations. It is evident that nations, states, and locations within states that have relatively high taxes also have lower growth and higher unemployment. The previous discussion about focusing on the local business environment is applicable when taxes are considered. Tax philosophy and application is a strong indicator of how supportive an area is for business. The local taxes and general business environment of an area is something that a person just moving into the working world should consider. You should choose a local market environment that is supportive of business by taxing its citizens and property owners at lower rates. This gives you a better chance to improve your freedom and increase your opportunity for happiness.

The one area that has not been covered in coping with the business/market environment is investments. This can affect you and your family in both the income and freedom/happiness philosophy areas. The current government thinking in many European nations and the United States not only believes in taxing heavily but also places high-cost operating burdens on businesses. Those countries' work rules, health insurance requirements, and legal systems place businesses at a disadvantage in competing with less developed countries. This makes it challenging for European and U.S. companies to compete in international markets without a technological edge on their competitors. Labor intensive businesses with mid to low skill employees are at a grave disadvantage. So how does an investor cope who either wants to own and operate a business in a developed country or who only wants to invest their funds from a developed country?

If you choose to operate your own business, these are some of the thoughts that you will have to consider under the current circumstances:

1.   Will there be full-time employees as part of the business?
2.   If there are full-time employees, what overhead will be associated with the business's operation?   Health insurance, retirement

plan, unemployment insurance, Social Security, and Medicare should be considered.

3. Are operating expenses less than projected revenues? Considering that energy expenses will increase with a carbon tax in the future, as will income taxes.

4. Can the business operate in a localized area that is not subject to competition from businesses located in low-cost foreign markets?

5. Is there growth in people and/or income in the local area?

6. Is there an unmet need or shortage of the products of the prospective business in the local area?

With all the above considerations satisfied and knowledge of the local business environment, you can gain freedom and the happiness of control over your business destiny.

If you choose to invest in businesses and companies that are operated by others, you will need to consider the following in the current business climate:

1. Is the business in an area with the strong support of tax policies, labor regulations, and benefit requirements that will encourage growth?

2. Is the business in a location where there is either strong demand for its product or service or it has a decided advantage over competitors in other locations?

3. Are there above-average growth prospects for the business in spite of rising national taxes and higher energy costs?

You improve your prospects when your money works for you instead of you working for money. Prudent investment can provide you additional income. With sufficient income, freedom can be gained from the burden of earning enough to provide basic requirements for living. In an area with high income taxes, the challenge of gaining higher investment income is increased. In high tax areas, it will be necessary to use investment strategies to minimize taxes on the derived income.

The large industrialized countries of Europe and the United States have allowed a financial crisis to exist that will take years to overcome. Without perfect foresight, it is not possible to say exactly how this crisis will play out. It is possible that there will be more deflation, as experienced in the fall of 2008. There will either be higher taxes and lower take-home pay, or there will be continuing taxes with higher pay and higher inflation. You must keep in mind the ultimate goal of greater freedom and increased opportunity for happiness. To accomplish that goal, you must remain flexible in your plans and actions over the next few years.

COPING WITH THE SOCIAL ENVIRONMENT

The world that we are now living in has become much more complicated than the one that our parents and ancestors experienced. Although it is natural that you would desire more freedom and happiness, the challenge of coping with an increasingly complex world has been overwhelming. In addition to the difficult world that you are experiencing, the leading industrial countries in the world have overextended themselves to provide more goods and services than is needed. The leadership of those countries have set examples that have filtered down to many of their citizens and created consumer economies. The consumer economies continued to encourage their citizens to purchase more goods and services, even as spending greatly exceeded incomes. While spending more than income works for countries that can print more money, it does not work for individuals. The result of this poor leadership is confusion in direction and low expectations for overcoming high debt burdens. This has happened over the last fifty or so years at such a gradual pace that it has been almost unnoticed. Now, the average citizen has debts that are high, while the prospects for increased income are low. The leaders of the countries that have allowed or encouraged this condition are now encouraging citizens to continue the practices that have led to this situation.

Individuals are now experiencing frustration and anger at their state of affairs, yet do not know how to change it. The spirit of freedom and independence that helped the leading countries increase their standards of living has diminished. The power of central governments has increased while the prospects of the citizens of those governments have fallen. People are more dependent on their governments to do more for them and less dependent upon their own abilities to provide for themselves. The misdirection and low quality of leadership in governments has left people with low expectations and increasing despair. People have lost their sense of self and are faced with simply reacting to events. Individuals and many of their leaders have come to depend on the various communications media for information and direction.

The fact that people who manage and participate in the various media sources are other citizens in the same environment is forgotten. No other individual knows better than themselves what and how events and decisions impact them.

The old adage of "Question Authority" applies, whether the authority is a media source, a fellow citizen, or political authorities. No one knows better than you what is best for you. You must question the objective of information given to the public. Today's world has almost an infinite source of information available from the Internet either through public facilities or from a personal computer. A way to test information gained through other sources should be through the Rotary Test:

1. Is it the TRUTH?
2. Is it FAIR to all concerned?
3. Will it build GOOD WILL and BETTER FRIENDSHIPS?
4. Will it be BENEFICIAL to all concerned?

Knowledge is a key to gaining the freedom and independence that has been lost over the last generation of citizens. Once you know what is important to yourself and your family, it makes it much easier to make decisions to gain more freedom.

If we are to make the necessary changes to improve the prospects of future generations, we must gain the freedom and independence of our parents and ancestors. It was much easier for your ancestors to be more independent in a simpler world. You can, however, view history to see that our ancestors had a much more hostile and environmentally challenging atmosphere to overcome. The number of people killed or displaced by conflicts of the past centuries was much higher than in today's world. The number of people who died in natural disasters and from diseases was also higher than currently experienced. The fact that we are here today is a testament to the efforts and abilities of our ancestors. It is important for people today to appreciate the efforts made by their forebears to make our existence possible. It is necessary for today's generation to make the same efforts that our ancestors made so that we can provide for future generations.

> *"We owe it to our ancestors to preserve entire those rights, which they have delivered to our care: we owe it to our posterity, not to suffer their dearest inheritance to be destroyed."*

Junius: Pseudonym of the author of a series of letters in the *London Public Advertiser* 1769–1771 published in book form in 1772. They have been attributed to, among others, Sir Philip Francis, Lord Shelburne, Lord George Sackville, and Lord Temple.

It is not enough to just appreciate what our ancestors did for us. We must, as the writer quoted above intends, revive the rights and freedoms given to us by our ancestors. This can only be done by each of us making an effort to gain our freedom and independence. This can be done by you in the following ways:

1. **Test communications:** Apply the Rotary Test to what you see, hear, and read. Question authority, the source, and the content to be sure that it is in your best interest. Think about media promotions for goods, services, or causes that may sound good, but do nothing to promote your freedom or independence.
2. **Define what is important:** Learn what is important to your life and direction in life by looking at your life. Do not depend on what others tell you is needed to meet their standards. Be careful not to place importance on goods and services that are more important to the people who are promoting those goods or services. You should not accept a good or service that may partly improve your situation. It may cost much more than you and your children can afford in future freedom and independence.

3. **Invest wisely in your future:** Invest your resources in goods, services, and causes that will improve both current and future freedom and independence for you and your family. Do not settle for brief happiness in return for future sacrifices and reduced happiness. Short-term grasping of perceived happiness has been the method by which the current outlook and prospects have developed.

We do not have the physically threatening environment that previous generations faced. We do have a much more complex environment, and this environment requires knowledge and use of the many resources that civilization has made available. We have a more technically and economically complicated atmosphere, but have more tools with which to work. We must handle the high stress of a complicated world like past generations handled the stress of a physically threatening world. We must use the many information and technology sources available to relieve the stress of ignorance to gain knowledge and rapid response.

The courage that our ancestors had to overcome the dangers that they faced is needed in today's world to overcome the complexities that confound and overwhelm us. We must find the courage to brave the barrage of information that is transmitted at us to sell goods, services, and causes. The media developed to improve communication and entertain often leads people to spend resources that sacrifice freedom for short-term happiness. The speed and volume of information has driven people to become reactive rather than proactive. As reactive people, they become easily used as pawns by advertisers of various products. It will take true bravery for you to disregard what is promoted as the popular opinion about a product to determine what is truly best for you and your family. Promotions for various products (whatever they may be) often try to convince people that their product is popular with the majority and that rivals are unpopular or ineffective.

If you are to gain the freedom to attain the happiness you want, it will take the bravery that your ancestors displayed in starting new lives and overcoming adversity. It will be a different kind of bravery because this is not a physically threatening world. Today's world will require the bravery in a social sense that past generations did not conceive. The reward will not be the reward of physical survival of past generations, but will be the reward of improved happiness for future generations.

COPING WITH YOUR MENTAL/EMOTIONAL ENVIRONMENT

As just mentioned in coping with the social environment, it will take courage for you to gain control of your life. It will be necessary for you to withstand media and peer pressures encouraging more consumption. You must choose what is best for yourself and your family. In carrying out this action, it will mean that in many groups with which you socialize, you will be "the odd person out." This will mean a number of things, including the following:

1. Avoiding events that simply consume time and funds to be with some people that you, at other times, would prefer not to be with
2. Not buying goods that others value for status, but do not add anything to your freedom or happiness
3. Saving your funds to invest in goods that improve your freedom and increase your ability to gain happiness
4. Supporting political candidates who promise to reduce spending for popular benefits of things that people should do for themselves
5. Using your time and resources to increase your knowledge and ability in order to improve your work opportunities
6. Promoting causes that increase individual freedom while reducing government expenses on popular programs that increase dependence

The examples above are but a few actions in which you will be involved to regain your independence and increase your freedom. Not only will it take courage, but it will take persistence and stubbornness. The challenge will be increased if you depend on the approval of those around you and the feeling of satisfaction in following the crowd.

*"Courage is to feel
The daily daggers of relentless steel
And keep on living"*

*Douglas Malloch (1877–1938), American
poet and syndicate writer*

For those who are strongly dependent upon the influence of others, it will be necessary to change the way they think and feel. It may mean being treated differently by people with whom you associate. It may mean losing popularity with people who had treated you with enjoyable times. It may mean finding new friends and acquaintances and finding new groups and organizations to which to belong. This can be a difficult adjustment for a socially involved individual, as it will be difficult mentally and emotionally to make adjustments to your social involvements.

The best method for coping with difficult mental and emotional conditions is to plan and prepare for those that you can imagine happening. Some of the actions that you can undertake would be the following:

1. Determine that independence and happiness is most important for yourself and your family. Consider that this will mean possible changes in your social environment and that of your family and that this will be an investment in their freedom and happiness.
2. Realize that it is not necessary to be public about your plans to increase your and your family's freedom and happiness. Assure that your family is equally informed of the need for privacy with regards to your plans. Assure that all the family understands the Rotary Test on what to say and do, yet it does not require crusades where different from publicly accepted beliefs.

3. Begin making changes in associations with those individuals in which you are in close and most frequent contact. Increase contact with those individuals with which you most agree on the need for increased freedom and an opportunity for happiness. Gradually decrease contact with those with whom you least agree on the need for increased freedom and an opportunity for happiness.

4. Begin making changes in organizations and community involvements that you feel have impacts on your community and family. Increase involvement in those organizations or clubs that you feel most increase individual freedom and the opportunity for happiness. Decrease involvement in those organizations and clubs that you feel least increase individual freedom and the opportunity for happiness.

5. Allot time to leisure and relaxing activities to assure some enjoyment in your life to secure a break from life's stresses. Freedom and happiness should be part of your normal life, not a challenging goal. For extroverted individuals, this could mean activities with other individuals who have similar beliefs, though differences in beliefs can be entertaining and educational. For those with more introverted personalities, there are entertaining and educational activities like reading, Internet browsing, painting, gardening, and photography.

6. To increase the enjoyment of moving toward a more independent and happy existence, reward yourself and your family after each major achievement. Set up a plan of goals that you want to achieve and how soon you would hope to reach them. When a goal is reached, reward yourself and your family appropriately with a joyous experience.

Moving courageously toward freedom and independence need not be a strain on your mental and emotional well-being. Quite the contrary, the more liberated you feel, the more enjoyment you will get from your life. The consumer society that generated stronger dependence upon central governments has failed the majority of the citizens within the industrialized countries. At first, it will take some bravery to move toward independence, but people will increase happiness as their efforts continue.

GAINING MORE FREEDOM AND
HAPPINESS FROM OUR ENVIRONMENTS

Whether you like to be involved or are more comfortable with little inter-action with others, you can multiply desired results by inclusion of or with others. Actions that help others to gain their goals can be done individu-ally or with a group. Single people acting alone can increase their power by joining with others in group actions or by doing their part to achieve the same end with solitary actions. The key for our world is to help others to either increase their freedom or to multiply their happiness. The more people involved in an objective, either working toward achieving it or benefitting from it, multiplies its value.

Using elections as an example can demonstrate how a single vot-er can multiply his or her impact to gain the objective of achieving a desired outcome. That single voter can work individually to publish articles and letters to the newspaper editors in support of a candidate or desired outcome. That same single voter can join with others to spon-sor or organize fundraising and/or supporting events to increase the popularity of the candidate or election outcome. Although elections are closely related to political systems that have recently led people away from freedom, this example shows that even solitary action can work to accomplish the same thing as group action.

Actions should focus on improving freedom to gain the opportunity for happiness. Improving freedom of individuals, groups, or organiza-tions allows all the freedom of choice to follow a direction that is most agreeable. When individuals, groups, or organizations gain the freedom that is part of their normal state, they gain a joy that is most natural. That natural joy of freedom is multiplied by the number of people expe-riencing it as they use their freedom to help those around them to gain and enjoy freedom. One needs only to experience seeing the joy of a group of children doing something together that they like to see how the joy of the group multiplies as each child begins to enjoy the action.

"The path to greatness is along with others."

Baltasar Gracian (1601–1658)
Spanish priest and popular writer

Just as Father Gracian states, the path to greater freedom is by working in the same direction as others. Success will come to those who find a way to multiply their efforts to achieve an end by combining their efforts with others. The greatness is in the multiple impact of action that joins with the actions and happiness of others.

"The superior man encourages the people at their work, and exhorts them to help one another."

I Ching: Book of Changes, China, c. 600 BC

The goal of freedom requires that each individual aspires to use that freedom to advance themselves in their search for happiness. It will take more than an individual effort to truly multiply that happiness beyond an internal feeling. By encouraging others and working with them, the joy experienced by a single person will be multiplied by the joy shared with others in common efforts.

As you address each of the different environments in your life, you can choose to improve your freedom as a single person. If that is your choice, it will be tackling the task the hard way. By working with others or working in cooperation with others, the chances for success will be increased, and the enjoyment of success will be increased. You can learn to cope with each major environment to increase your ability to gain the freedom to improve your happiness. If you want to make major progress beyond the ability to cope with each environment, it will take an effort that coordinates and cooperates with others. With this type of attempt, it will be possible to improve your freedom and opportunity for happiness and help others achieve the multiplied benefits of a free and happy life.

IMPROVING OUR RELIGIOUS/SPIRITUAL ENVIRONMENT

There are countries, parts of countries, and groups within countries that are not following God's commandments by their actions to harm people outside of their area or group. There is no good reason why harm, or even death, of one group should be desired by another. Individuals or groups of individuals that wish to harm others do not want to allow freedom of others to make choices in their lives. To improve this environment, each individual involved will need to work toward improving their own thinking and immediate environment. There cannot be joy or happiness if a person cannot freely be allowed to follow the commandments themselves. Once people are able to act freely in a positive way, they can work on improving the thinking and actions of those with whom they are involved.

You can only improve your religious/spiritual environment if you decide that your present environment does not give you the joy and happiness you need. You should feel comfortable with the beliefs and activities of your current religion or spiritual direction. Your religion or spiritual beliefs should make you comfortable in your dealings with others. Following God's commandments should allow you to feel comfort in dealings with others, whether a member of a certain religion or not. Limited individuals who do not believe in God must still believe in themselves and the life that they were given by their parents. Whatever religion or spiritual belief that you have must place the highest importance on the freedom given to you at birth. It is up to you to make the most of that freedom to improve your life.

Freedom is certainly not a religion, but it is fundamental to your spirit. Freedom, with which you are born, can be and should be used to follow the commandments. That freedom should be used to make life's choices to follow the commandments to live in harmony with the world around us. Choosing to live in harmony with the rest of the world must be done of free will and not to follow the dictates of a particular religion or political philosophy. By using free will in relations with others and in accord with the commandments, you gain the advantage of life with reduced chances of conflicts (a peaceful life).

Reduced chances of conflicts is a good goal for improving your religious/spiritual environment, but it only gives you an opportunity to live without conflicts. It may be enough for many to only avoid conflict, while living a good life in agreement with the commandments. Greater satisfaction and joy in life can come from religious and spiritual relationships with others. Whether your relation with others is one-on-one or through organizations or groups, the results can be multiplied by the number of others that you can help. There are several ways that you can help others improve their religious/spiritual environment:

- Freedom education: by helping others to see that they were born with freedom and liberty and that they can gain freedom and independence
- Improving freedom: by helping others to see that they have freedom of choice in their lives and that they have choices other than their current beliefs
- Multiplying joy: by helping others to see that they can use their freedom to follow the commandments and can gain by helping others

You can make the most of your gifts from birth through interaction with others. Interactions that can be coordinated with others can multiply the benefits for each person involved. Coordination can be done through a wide range of actions, ranging from one-on-one relations to group or organization relations.

You can work with one person at a time or can work in groups or organizations to help others seek freedom and use that freedom to improve their spiritual environment. In one-on-one relationships, you can work through your most common interactions, such as work, organization, and friends and family relations. In those relationships, you can remind others that, as human beings, we were born free and that it is normal for humans to desire to be free. Slavery was long ago abolished by most civilized countries. It is important that you seek to gain as much freedom and liberty as you can within the laws of your country. This means that, as free individuals, you are not slaves to a religion, political ideology, or the dictates of other organizations in which you are allowed some freedom of choice. You can help close relationships see the opportunity to gain freedom and escape the slavery of an ideology that restricts their independence.

Members of social organizations that are affiliated with religious organizations have the advantage of acceptance of the commandments and the condemnation of slavery. It is up to you to help the other members to understand that freedom is making independent choices in their lives. Following a path to help others in their choices will multiply the increase in their happiness. It is most likely that religiously related organizations will want to help others. It will be good to educate fellow members of such organizations on the multiplication of the benefits in helping others without political reasons. The importance of the work of such organizations is in their efforts to help others become more independent.

An individual who is not affiliated with a religion, or is entirely not religious, can still benefit from helping others in a spiritual sense. Whether individuals are limited or not, they can follow the last six commandments and maintain high moral standards in dealing with others. A person unaffiliated with a religion can also help others by working with groups that help people become more independent. Those organizations may or may not be religiously oriented. Whether the organization is religiously oriented or not, individuals can help orient it to the importance of increasing freedom and independence of the people that they try to help. The unaffiliated person gains spiritual benefits from the satisfaction in helping others achieve freedom and independence. The spiritual benefit will be multiplied by the number of people helped and will benefit all involved in the group effort.

If you choose to work with others in a religious or spiritual environment to improve others' freedom and opportunity for happiness, you can gain both satisfaction and happiness. Whether the work done is one-on-one or through a group, there is the psychic gain of working with others to do something good. There can be no doubt that improving others' freedom and opportunity for happiness will provide happiness and satisfaction. You can be assured that successful efforts in this environment will fulfill the condition of freedom with which you were born and what your parents will have wanted.

Individual efforts done in coordination with others will be able to improve the actions of countries, parts of countries, and groups within countries to allow freedom of choice. Those efforts will also improve the opportunity to gain happiness for the people within those groups. This type of effort has just begun in some of the Middle Eastern countries. As more people become involved in spreading freedom and the opportunity for happiness, the relations between countries and groups within countries will improve. Harm and conflicts can be reduced to provide a more peaceful existence for large numbers of people and countries. The peaceful existence will then free those people to seek happiness and to raise the level of happiness for those with whom they associate. As more individuals and groups coordinate their efforts, not only will their level of happiness increase, but the level of happiness will be multiplied by the number of people involved.

IMPROVING OUR POLITICAL/GOVERNMENT ENVIRONMENT

The national governments of most of Europe and the United States have experienced slow or negative growth in their economies. The economic environments of those countries have high and/or rising unemployment and are running budgets with higher expenses than revenues (deficits). The cause of these poor performances is the governments themselves. Those governments adopted economic policies that allowed their central banks to increase the supply of money and support low interest rates that totally distorted the free market. This distortion allowed and encouraged risk taking by large financial institutions and real estate-related companies to expand beyond even a high free-market level of operation. The Internet and real estate bubbles in the United States were the result of political management by the Federal Reserve of interest rates and the money supply. The damage to the economy of the United States can be measured in lost jobs, lower stock prices, higher personal and national debt, and a lower standard of living for many citizens.

One can only wonder how the three branches of government (executive, legislative, and judicial) have allowed the Federal Reserve to gain economic power greater than any of them. A lack of leadership by those three branches allowed it to create conditions that did such tremendous damage to the U.S. economy and to the world. If there is going to be an improvement to the political/government environment, citizens must regain the power of representation within the government. Short of a revolution, it will take strong, decisive action to find and elect people that will represent them in Congress and to assure judicial appointees that move government power back closer to the citizens. The people must elect members of Congress with the following qualities:

1. Understanding of how the economy, the money supply, and the free market work. Jobs, income, and business activity in a free market are keys to citizens' welfare and must be understood by

representatives at the local, state, and national levels to avoid market "bubbles."

2. The guts to make decisions that use economic and common sense to provide programs that increase freedom rather than dependence. Decisions must be based upon sound economics and common sense rather than attempting to buy votes without regard to realistic expectations.

3. The integrity and moral courage to speak truthfully and straight to citizens to assure them that the government cannot solve all their problems. Although it is easier to reduce people's risk and provide better security, people must be allowed to fail or succeed based on their own free choices.

The last two years have emphasized the importance of the relationship between government and business. Improving how the government/political environment works will require a major change in direction from these issues:

1. The growth in national government power and influence at the expense of state and local power where citizens have more influence

2. The growth in the power of the Federal Reserve System and increase in the influence of major financial institutions at the expense of the citizens of the nation

3. The wasted resources of the national government in pursuing programs that reduce short-term risks to increase long-term obligations (debts) to be paid back by the next generations

4. Electing government representatives based upon promises without economical or common sense solutions instead of support of the free market business environment

5. Promoting government as being a means of transferring wealth from wealthy people to not wealthy people, instead of freeing more people to have the opportunity to become wealthy

6. Depending upon government to take actions and make decisions that are each individual's responsibility

All of the above changes will get the country back to what the founding fathers wanted for the country and what made the country the most powerful and wealthy country up until the 1960s. The last five decades have seen the United States become a debtor nation, more dependent each year on other countries to help fund its operation. This condition, due to recent skyrocketing deficit spending to aid large financial institutions, has placed a burden on the country that will not be overcome for many years. Congress has also wasted resources in providing services for U.S. citizens that they could have provided for themselves and has depleted the country's wealth by managing foreign affairs. The United States is now faced with increasing taxes on its citizens in order to continue to provide existing services. U.S. citizens now face rising taxes, high unemployment, and unstable home prices. This mismanagement is why there must be major changes in the national government environment.

Making changes to the national government funding will not cure the deteriorating financial and economic conditions of the citizens of a nation. Much waste is caused by "unfunded mandates." These measures are regulations and requirements passed or set at the national level. They generate expenses and restrictions at the state, local, or citizen levels without showing any expenses at the national level. Sneaking expenses into state, local, and citizen operations must be eliminated. It cannot simply be eliminated at the congressional level, but must also be addressed at all government levels. Members of Congress are often elected after working their way up the ladder from local and state level government positions. Representatives at all levels of government must be found and elected that assert and support the state, local, and citizens' interests to limit the national government's power. The federal or national government's authority must be limited only to its accountability and direct responsibility. The national government should not take credit for programs' results created without lower government levels or citizens' representation. Before a program becomes national, state and local governments should have to pass approval of any programs for which they must either charge fees or collect taxes.

It is easy to find fault in the workings of various government bureaucracies, because many running for office have little ability other than the ambition to gain votes by promising benefits with other people's funds (taxes at state and local level). At the national level of government, the ability to print money has allowed the national government to expand benefits far beyond what can be funded by taxes or revenues. This uncontrolled management of funding of the national budget has resulted in increased growth in the power of the national government. This has also resulted in greater dependence of its citizens on the services it provides. As the dependence on the national/federal government has increased, so has the debt that this and future generations will have to pay in taxes and/or inflation. As time goes on and the mismanagement of the levels of government continues, the citizens continue to pay a higher price for temporary benefits.

The continuation of the growth in power of the national government and the loss of power of the state and local governments is a loss of freedom for you. Greater dependence on the government, while taxes increase, reduces your choices and freedom. As mismanagement of the government eventually increases inflation, this reduces the amount of income available to spend as you see fit. Just as each person must pay a part of their income for taxes, they must look at those taxes as an investment. With those taxes now reducing the freedom to gain happiness, individual citizens are realizing a negative return on their investment. To put it clearly, tax-paying citizens are losing money on their investment in government. **NATIONAL GOVERNMENT GROWTH REDUCES FREEDOM AND IS A NEGATIVE RETURN ON YOUR TAXES.**

What can you do to improve this situation? A single person cannot make the changes necessary. A single member of Congress, president, or cabinet member cannot make the changes necessary to gain government action to increase freedom and the chance for happiness to citizens. The effort must come from actions by people willing to work together in coordinated actions. A great example for people to follow is the "Tea Parties" that have been put together by thousands of people in the United States. These actions are much similar to those taken by citizens in the American colonies. Both actions and the goal that they sought were to gain freedom so that people could choose what would best make them happy. In the seventeen hundreds, it may have been necessary to take up arms and risk lives to gain freedom and the opportunity to be happy. In today's modern environment, it should not be necessary to take up arms. There are ways that we can regain the freedom that drove the United States to become the economically strong country that provided the best opportunities in the world for its citizens. To make the necessary changes in government, we must take the following actions:

1. **Multiply time and efforts by joining with others:** Single individuals have little influence on elections or on actions by elected officials. The first and most important effort must be using your time and energy to support your cause. By joining others at local, state, regional, and national levels, you can gain influence from the numbers in your group or organization. Governments are run by elected officials or managers who work for those officials. Today's technology gives people the tools to identify like-minded people and multiply their efforts. You can use a search of the Internet for political action groups that support freedom like www.freedomscall.org. You can also join local actions groups in the area to find others to add numbers your cause by using www.facebook.com to get others to join your efforts. You can also use a site like www.grassroots.com to develop a cause and promote your group's views. It is also possible to work within the major political parties to move them to a political philosophy that gives more emphasis to a freedom philosophy. The political parties of various countries and the United States can be found on the Internet. The party most in line with the freedom and happiness philosophy is the Libertarian Party and found at www.lp.org. To be truly effective, you must find others with which to work in order

to influence elections and the actions of those elected. Maximum results can be obtained by finding organizations with which you agree and then investing your time and energy to strengthen the issues that you support. Working through the Internet and organizations on it uses little time, yet can be most effective and efficient in the use of precious time. With only a few hours a week, you can increase your influence on elections and government actions. The efficiency of working this way gives you the choice of using more than one site and working on various levels of government. Your efforts can be further multiplied by using several sites.

2. **Multiply funding efforts by joining with others:** You have limited resources in which to invest in a cause or issue. Once you decide that you prefer **FREEDOM AND HAPPINESS**, the first investment that you will need to make is your precious time and efforts. With today's technology, you can accomplish much with little time and effort invested by joining with others. To invest more than time and effort in an issue or philosophy, you may fund organizations that support your beliefs. Considering the future of your family gives high rank to investment in groups and causes that support freedom and opportunity for happiness. The strategy for investment simply pits reducing government intrusion and low return on investment versus positive return on the future for yourself and your children.

3. **Focus education efforts on freedom issues:**

   a. **Regulating and limiting financial institution risks:** These are the poor regulatory and weak lending practices that caused the depression of the 1930s and the financial problems that started in the last decade. Bad lending practices were encouraged by poor Federal Reserve oversight and congressional regulation that allowed higher leverage on home loans. The higher leverage meant that in some cases financial institutions were able loan up to forty times the amount of assets for which they were responsible. That means that only 2.5 percent of loans failing caused financial institutions to lose money and restricted their ability to make future loans. Control over money supply and interest rates helps the Federal Reserve control citizens' spending and debt to the benefit of large financial institutes. This takes away your freedom and increases your dependence on paying debts to large financial institutions. It also increases dependence on the federal/national government for basic needs that you should be able to provide for yourself. You should only support political organizations and candidates that:

i.   Believe in auditing and limiting Federal Reserve operations to oversight from Congress and the Treasury Department until its operations become part of the Treasury Department

ii.   Believe in limiting control of money supply and interest rates to the Treasury, with congressional audit of Treasury operations

iii.   Believe in moving all money supply and interest rate operations from the Federal Reserve to the Treasury Department

iv.   Believe in mortgages and business loans leverage being limited to a multiple of savings deposits that is regulated by the Treasury Department

v.   Believe that Congress should set definite limits on how large the multiple should be for mortgage and business loans over savings deposits

vi.   Believe that banks and financial institutions should be allowed to fail and only depositors given limited protection

b. Limiting the federal/national government authority:
Limits the national government authority to the extent
that they can fund regulations with taxes and revenues
at the national level. Unfunded mandates from
representatives, who are not responsible to local desires
or objectives, would be eliminated without national
funding. The country would be responsible for balancing its budget, as are most states, counties, and cities
in the United States. Government at the national level
would be responsible for funding its programs within
realistic budgets. It cannot depend on simply printing
currency to make up for spending more than can be supported by revenues or free-market financing. The constant devaluing of national currency (money) that robs
average citizens of the ability to live within their budgets could be stopped. False hopes of happiness from
programs that enslave individuals to dependence on a
national government for basic needs could be stopped.
The freedom and control over individual lives can be
brought back to state and local governments where
people have more power. You should only support organizations and political candidates who believe in the
following:

     i.   Balanced budgets at the national level, without
consideration of unfunded mandates to states,
counties, or local governments

     ii.   Increased authority of state and local govern-
ments and less authority at the national/federal
level

     iii.   Supporting federal and local judges that limit na-
tional/federal authority and increasing state and
local authority

c. **Limiting government budgets to universal needs:** Limits on what and how much is spent on providing what all citizens need. This means that individuals are allowed to support their basic needs with their own efforts. Individuals will be free to provide for their food, income, clothing, shelter, and medical care by themselves. The first national government had only four cabinet members—the Attorney General, the Secretary of State, the Secretary of Treasury, and the Secretary of War or Defense. As the authority of the federal government grew and the authority of the state and local governments was lost, the number of cabinet members grew to fifteen. Because of their ability to create money to meet expanded budgets, the growth in power of the central government increased with their budgets. With virtually no limits on budgets at the national level, bureaucracy grew by creating a new department to address each perceived need. Representatives at the national level were able to create a new bureaucratic operation to attempt to cure every need or want. As a result, the national government has grown far beyond its ability to pay for all over which it has authority. Along with limits on authority of the national government, there must be limits on the budgets of the national government. With balanced budgets at the national level, realistic responsibilities would be passed down to state and local governments. This will also limit the time and expense with which people are burdened due to uncontrolled national government. The government needs to move to functions that provide the following:

    i.   Legal and judicial order
   ii.   Coordination between levels of government
  iii.   National and local defense and protection

    iv.   Taxing, treasury, and finance

    v.   Commerce coordination between nations, states, counties, and cities

There would be a limit on government providing services that free individuals should be able to provide for themselves. In the case of rare natural disasters, governments should be capable of providing short-term aid to people involved. You should only support organizations and political candidates who believe in the following:

1. Limiting the national/federal government authority and giving more authority to the state and local governments—and the citizens

2. Managing the economy through the Treasury and Commerce operations controlled by the president and Congress

3. Balanced budgets at all levels that limit government spending to services that benefit all citizens and that builds a surplus to aid in case of natural disasters

4. Limiting defense and protection budgets to defense of the citizens represented by that level of government

5. Allowing the free market and free choice to determine the value of goods and services without subsidies

6. Minimal taxing of all citizens at the same rate, without discrimination

The central/federal government has become oversized, inefficient, and ineffective because the Federal Reserve and the large financial institutions that control it were allowed to gain too much power over the economy. The free market has been overcome by an oversized central government. The strength in the economy gained in the two centuries before the 1960s was due to the free market presence allowed by state and local government operations. The growth in the economy and jobs was due to the diversity and competition between states and local communities that drove them to exceed. This produced growth in business, jobs, and prosperity for U.S. citizens. The power of the citizens of the United States must be allowed to return, so that economic growth, jobs, and prosperity can return. This can only be done by freeing people and businesses to seek happiness as only they know how, without an intrusive, restrictive government.

> *"Those who won our independence believed that the final end of the State was to make men free to develop their faculties; and that in its government the deliberative forces should prevail over the arbitrary. They valued liberty both as an end and as a means. They believed liberty to be the secret of happiness and courage to be the secret of liberty."*
>
> *Louis D. Brandeis (1856-1941), Supreme Court Justice*

As many know, government moves slowly. In the case of bad government, slow is in the citizens' best interests. Improving government will be slower than most would want. With elections spread over years, it will take a long time if the changes are made one election at a time. Politicians who are truly public servants will, however, notice the messages that are sent by blocks of voters and by politically active organizations. You should count on continuing efforts that will gradually be noticed by the politicians and the media. With your efforts that are joined by others, the government can be made to serve its citizens by bringing back your freedom and giving you the opportunity for happiness.

IMPROVING OUR LEGAL/JUDICIAL ENVIRONMENT

The legal/judicial system does not work on a purely logical basis. The system is composed of people, and people are not perfect. In theory, the courts interpret and judge opposing arguments in a case or issue using existing laws or precedents from decisions in previous court cases. As people are different, so will their interpretation of existing laws and decisions in prior court cases. In criminal cases, there is less likely to be as much difference in interpretation between different courts as in civil court cases. In some areas, judges are elected by citizens in their jurisdiction. In other areas, judges are appointed by government office holders. In the case of appointed judges, the government official who appoints the judge must gain approval from a wider group of officeholders. An example would be U.S. Supreme Court judges who are appointed by the president, but must get congressional confirmation. Whether judges are elected or appointed, citizens in their jurisdiction can have an influence on who becomes a judge and how court cases are judged. Obviously, individuals can vote for the type of judge that they want and how they feel that the judge will act in court. For judges who are appointed, people can elect representatives who will support their views on court actions. Those representatives can in turn influence who is approved for judge positions and what type of rulings that those judges will make.

All the above is the general view of the mechanics of the judicial system. The operation of the judicial system has followed a trend that has changed from what the writers of the Constitution of the United States had in mind. Over the years, some of the judgments by the courts in the United States have resulted in the following:

1. Strengthening the national/federal government and reducing the authority and influence of state, county, and local governments where people have the most influence
2. Reducing freedom and increasing restrictions on businesses where jobs are created and incomes generated

3. Reinforcing a more complex system of laws with rulings supporting those laws that attempt to aid small factions at the expense of the majority of citizens
4. Allowing increased ease in pursuit of civil actions that produce settlements depending less on interpretations of laws and more on perceived or liberally interpreted opinions
5. Easing the variety of types and subjects of civil actions
6. Easing the level of settlements on civil actions

The evolution of the legal/judicial system in the United States has resulted in a complex system that is increasingly more difficult within which to function. The growth of the authority of the federal government has generated more laws and regulations to address any perceived need that may affect a citizen. The laws and regulations that begin at the federal level translate and generate additional laws and regulations at the state and local levels of government. The growth into a complex, confusing system of laws and regulations has caused the following results:

1. Increased cost of government at all levels to administer the laws and regulations
2. Increased probability and possibility of lawsuits
3. Increased need for insurance
4. Increased cost of doing business
5. Decreased growth of businesses
6. Decreased opportunity for nongovernment jobs

There is no doubt that people must have laws and order to have the opportunity to gain freedom and function within that freedom to gain happiness. Order can enhance and support freedom. Laws and regulations should not generate confusion and unwarranted inhibitions. The legal/judicial system needs to be improved to serve citizens in a simplified, more practical direction. You should only back candidates or organizations in support of those political candidates will do the following:

a. Will appoint or support appointments of judges who will give more authority to state or local governments rather than the federal or national government
b. Will appoint or support appointments of judges who will favor the free market business economy
c. Will appoint or support appointments of judges who believe in truly equal and fair treatment of all citizens, regardless of race, color, religion, or sexual orientation
d. Will appoint or support appointments of judges who believe in unsuccessful litigants paying all legal costs
e. Will appoint or support appointments of judges who believe in requiring clearly measurable and definable harm in civil actions
f. Will appoint or support appointments of judges who believe in settlements of civil actions based on clearly realistic, definable damages rather than punitive assessments

It will take years of effort to gain improvements in the legal/judicial system because some judges are appointed for life. In addition, it is at least as difficult to unseat an in-place judge as an in-place member of Congress. Those of you who want to make improvements to the system can hope that in-place judges will be influenced by the type of appointments and elections that are successful at making improvements. Although it may take some time, the direction toward a simplified and practical legal/judicial system can be obtained with the combined and concentrated efforts of concerned, active citizens. With an orderly, improved system, the freedom of individuals, governments, and businesses will allow them to grow, create jobs, and find happiness.

IMPROVING THE BUSINESS/MARKET ENVIRONMENT

The present business environment is characterized by high unemployment with high levels of government spending and increased central government control of business activity. Two of the top three U.S. auto manufacturers have been taken over by the government. Many of the large banks owe their survival to government bailout funds. Many small banks have failed. Business loans are very difficult to obtain. The central government of the United States is attempting to gain additional control of the energy and medical markets while increasing the need for higher taxes. The impression given by the federal government is that more government involvement in business is necessary. It appears as though the U.S. government feels as though it should become more like the European governments. Those governments' economies normally and regularly were outperformed by the U.S. economy. The cause of the current poor performance of the U.S. economy is the poor management of the Federal Reserve and the failure of the federal government to control its actions. Giving the Federal Reserve and that same government more control over the economy will result in more of the same ills.

The Federal Reserve was established in the early years of the 1900s. It gained strength over the years, even though it may have been responsible for the Great Depression. The Federal Reserve gained strength as the large banks that have the most influence on its operations gained strength. Those banks gained strength because the economy of the United States gained strength, especially after World War II. With the help of court rulings, the Federal Reserve gained more independence from the central government. Over time, the Federal Reserve continued to gain power. This was due to independence from the central government, growing strength of the major financial institutions, and the dollar becoming the world reserve currency after World War II. When President Richard Nixon dropped the final official level of gold backing for the dollar, the Federal Reserve gained ultimate power over the economy. That power and with the dollar as the world reserve currency (meaning it is the basis of value in all business transactions in the world) allowed the Federal

Reserve to fund national budgets by creating currency (dollars). It also meant that other countries would help fund U.S. deficits by buying the country's notes and bonds. As more dollars were printed without any real backing, it meant that the dollar would be able to buy less of real goods (fuel, food, clothing, and housing) called inflation. As long as the U.S. created currency no faster than other countries, the dollar's value did not decrease versus other currencies, and all countries experienced inflation.

Inflation only gets out of control in a country when it creates currency faster than other countries (recent experience in Zimbabwe and Germany after WWI). In recent years, the United States and its European neighbors have had to increase the creation of their currency at a faster pace to pay for aid to the large financial institutions. Countries like China, Brazil, India, Russia, and the Arab nations that supply most of the real goods have had to create their currencies at similar rates. This allowed them to purchase more of the U.S. and European debt to keep from inflating the value of their own currencies. The supplying nations are trading their real goods and services for the rapidly increasing currencies of the consumer countries of the United States and Europe. This type of trade off is an acceptable business practice in an economic system with normally changing supply and demand factors. It is not an acceptable practice to trade goods of value for pieces of paper with no real value other than faith. It is only a matter of time and patience before goods-supplying countries either require real goods in trade or reduce their purchase of consumer countries' debt.

If the consumer countries are unable to supply real goods in exchange for the supplier countries' goods, the supplier countries will reduce their shipments to the consumer countries to equal the value of the consumer countries' goods. With fewer goods shipped by the producer/supplier countries to the consumer countries, the citizens of the consumer country will either pay a higher price for the limited supply or will reduce consumption. Reducing consumption beyond what is considered absolutely necessary is considered a lower standard of living. This means that the citizens of the consumer countries will either pay more for what they consume or reduce their standard of living.

If the consumer countries debt is not purchased at the same level by the supplier countries, the consumer countries must raise the interest rate on their debt to lure the supplier/producer countries to purchase their debt. As the interest rate on the consumer country's debt increases, the cost of the consumer country's government will also increase. As the cost of the consumer country's government increases, the consumer country's government can either print more money or raise taxes to pay its bills. Printing more money will increase inflation and the cost of necessities. Raising taxes reduces the sum of money that people have to spend on necessities. This means that consumer countries' citizens will either pay more for what they consume or reduce what they spend on necessities (a reduction in the standard of living).

All the above verbiage is to lead the reader to see how we have gotten to where we are at present. The citizens of the United States and European countries are in consumer countries. The governments of the consumer countries have expanded the supply of their currencies at a tremendous pace since the fall of 2008. The supplier/producer countries are approaching a time limit on how long they will continue to fund the consumption of the consumer countries. The supplier/producers are giving up the valuable resources of labor, oil, copper, iron, and assorted raw materials in return for the dwindling value of currencies that are rapidly approaching a zero value.

Some citizens of the consumer countries have lost homes, autos, and other possessions to their lenders. As will the supplier/producers act on the loans of resources that they have given to the United States and European countries. If the course of the consumer countries is not changed, **THE CHOICE WILL BE INFLATION OR A LOWER STANDARD OF LIVING.**

As described in the above history, we have not reached the current situation in only the last year or two. This environment has developed slowly and has just recently become obvious because the Federal Reserve and large financial institutions allowed risk to go too far. Congress and several presidents looked the other way because the risk that was allowed helped fund their political campaigns. It also allowed them to continue to provide more benefits and lower risks for citizens. This also increased the authority of the central government. That increased authority translated to more dependence on the central government. Much of the belief in more reliance and dependence upon the central government is something that has evolved over the last fifty years. The citizens allowed this to happen because it seemed natural since the country became so economically strong after World War II and could thus provide more for its citizens. During the last fifty years, the citizens of a great country became more dependent and less responsible for their own welfare as the free market faded. The citizens of the United States had gained strength and independence by overcoming trials of wars and economic adversities over the two centuries after its establishment. Some of that strength and independence has been lost, and all is in danger of being lost.

The central or federal government can get the country out this state of affairs. It will need to make the bold and brave changes that were made by the founders of the United States. The economy must be returned to the free market by the country's citizens. This is not the direction that the United States is currently heading. It will require a change in each of us and the cooperation of many working together to bring about the needed change. The changes must be made through altering the government and judicial environments that have the broad influence on how we live. The future of each of us and our families depends on the success of bringing about the change in those environments. The following will be required of each of us for the success of changing the direction of the United States and other consumer countries:

1. Each of us must improve our own personal independence by doing these things:
   a. Reducing the required level of necessary resources (food, clothing, shelter, and medical care)
   b. Looking at the risk in your income sources and reduce risks
   c. Saving for job/income changes or emergency expenses

    d. Gaining more skills and abilities to diversify income

    e. Developing and/or increase other income sources

    f. Considering alternative income sources or a job with lower risk

2. Each of us must reduce government dependence as much as possible to minimize risk of losing its help.

3. Each of us must consider and plan for the likelihood of increased taxes and reduced take-home pay.

4. Each of us must improve the thinking of the government by joining others to elect progressive, free market legislators and members of Congress.

5. Each of us must improve the thinking of the legal/judicial system by joining others to elect progressive legislators and members of Congress who will appoint or support free market judgments.

6. Each of us and the groups to which we belong must support local industries and the local government in dealing with those industries to encourage growth and job creation.

The individual citizens were the last to know that the economic system was moving toward a crisis until they were hit by the changes. You will not know if the needed changes work in the government and legal/judicial systems until jobs and opportunities start to increase. You will need to work with your fellow citizens in groups and organizations to help make the changes necessary for you and your families. It will be necessary for you to first gain independence for yourself before the free market can be achieved for all. With patience and success of organized efforts in the government and legal/judicial environments, you will gain continuing freedom and happiness for you and your families. Changes in people and thinking in the government and judicial environments will have to be accomplished before the free market is returned. When those changes develop, the free market will bring back the growth in business, the jobs that growing business provides, and an improved opportunity for happiness.

IMPROVING THE SOCIAL ENVIRONMENT

The industrialized countries experienced growth, improving oppor-tunities, and generally positive attitudes during the growth period of 1982 to 2007. Over the last two years, the mood has changed from positive outlooks to a feeling of confusion and frustration. People feel that things are not getting better, but do not know what they can do, or what their leaders can do, to make things better. There have always been ups and downs in countries' economies and in the general feel-ings of their populations during those times. The overriding trend from the early 1980s has been positive as interest rates gradually fell and the overall economies improved. The general direction and outlook of people in the developed countries improved as their risks were reduced. This happened as the Federal Reserve gradually reduced interest rates. Dependence on the national governments also increased as a result.

The mood of people has changed over the last couple of years as the real estate bubble burst. As a main source of wealth shrank, people's source of financial credit fell and was finally crushed with the second large stock bubble bursting in the last ten years. This left people with a feeling of reduced wealth and loss of confidence in their future. With loss of wealth and little credit available, individuals and businesses did not see a road to a better future. Government funds were focused on aiding large financial institutions and little aid reached the individual and citizen's business levels. The resulting feeling and mood of citizens is confusion and frustration over their lack of control of their future.

The solution by the U.S. government is more spending by the gov-ernment and encouraging more spending by its citizens. In addition, the U.S. government is proposing vastly expanding a health care system that is essentially broke and imposing additional taxes. The debt of the coun-try and its citizens will be increased at the same time that the cost of liv-ing for individuals and businesses increases. Those citizens who are able to see the future are fearful and concerned. They are most concerned with the outlook for jobs and spendable income of their own, their par-ents, their children, and grandchildren. The dependence on the central government and the reduction of risk for citizens and businesses was replaced by loss of confidence and fear and confusion about the future.

The Federal Reserve and the developed European countries with whom it coordinates have not provided a direction for a sustainable recovery. Building debts that will take funds away from their citizens and businesses is not a strategy to build lasting industries and the jobs they supply. People and businesses will need to regain the positive traits and actions present during the strong growth years of the United States. Independence and the ability to use the economic markets without government constraints are some of the characteristics that fostered personal and business growth. People must gain the freedom and independence necessary to choose a better path to improve their lives and the economic environment in which they live.

The gap between where people and businesses are versus the freedom and independence needed for better lives is too great to be accomplished by individuals. Improvement will start with each person, but to make the changes necessary it will take joint efforts on a broad scale. The same efforts that individuals need to gain their own independence must be joined with others to achieve the freedom necessary. That means that you will need to join with others who do the following:

1. **Test and question all:** Assure that what you and your organizations communicate promotes freedom and independence rather than persuading you and your organization to greater dependence and greater debt.

2. **Define what is important:** Assure that what you and your organizations seek will provide lasting improvements to freedom and independence rather than short-term benefits and greater dependence.

3. **Invest wisely:** Assure that the issues and causes in which you and your organizations invest time and efforts improve freedom and independence rather than buying short-term benefits and greater dependence.

The above methods will need to be applied to specific goals that give each person confidence that there will be an improvement in the direction of their lives and the country. These are some of the goals that people can share in their joint actions:

1. **Increased freedom for individuals:**
   a. Freedom from dependence on government by individuals for basic necessities that they are able to provide for themselves
   b. Freedom from prosecution for victimless crimes for adult individuals capable of making their own free choices
   c. Freedom from legal actions that lack measureable and clearly definable damages or criminal law basis
   d. Freedom from legal fees in defense of unsuccessful legal actions
   e. Freedom to act and speak freely without measurably offending another individual or groups of individuals
2. **Stronger voice in government** by reducing the authority of federal/national government so that government can be accountable to local and state values, while eliminating unfunded federal/national mandates.
3. **Balanced budgets at all government levels** by expecting all levels to balance budgets as done in states and localities to minimize government debts and increased taxes that result.
4. **Stronger national economy** by elimination of the Federal Reserve to make the Treasury, Congress, and the president chiefly responsible for the national economy. They will create money, set interest rates, and maintain a balanced budget as done in states and localities.
5. **Increased freedom in business and markets** by making governments responsible for supporting and allowing free markets, without any company or organization controlling the market for a good or service.

The above goals are mostly applicable to the improvements that were given for the government and legal/judicial environments. As in those environments, it will be necessary to use the Internet to find organizations compatible with people's goals. They can use the social networking sites to aid communications within those organizations. The importance of people feeling that there is something that can be done will help reduce the fear, clear up the confusion, and ease the frustration that has developed. With a strong joint effort, people can gain their freedom and some control toward the opportunity for happiness.

IMPROVING THE MENTAL/EMOTIONAL ENVIRONMENT

In coping with your mental/emotional environment, you will have gained some freedom by doing these things:

1. Supporting representatives and issues favoring freedom from government dependence
2. Improving opportunities through practical investment of personal time and resources
3. Improving life by avoiding wasted resources on short-term benefits and status and instead investing in increased freedom

The social environment can be helpful in coping with the thoughts and feelings that many feel in the current general external environment. Confusion and frustration are reduced when you believe that you are sharing those feelings with others. Though you may gain comfort in knowing that you are not alone, you still lack a direction that provides freedom to gain any happiness. Success in improving your social environment will aid your mental/emotional state, if you can join with others to work toward your goals. Joining with others of a like mind to move toward desired goals will give you a positive direction in your life and confidence in your future.

You can take the following actions through joint efforts to build on the freedom gained through singular efforts to improve the mental/emotional environment:

1. Networking with others in sites and groups that support and spread freedom efforts
2. Gaining comfort with the use of those groups and sites
3. Finding people or issues with which one is interested within the groups or sites
4. Involving family in groups, sites, issues, and relationships
5. Developing ways to celebrate achievements with contacts from groups and sites

6. Developing ways to reward family for achievements from groups and/or sites

The above actions will help to give a positive effort to you, your family, and the people with whom you have relations. The joint efforts in which you participate can give the following multiple benefits:

1. Sharing achievements, thoughts, and rewards through use of Facebook and other social networking sites with contacts and family
2. Returned benefits from others to whom you supplied aid
3. Sharing gains for each person involved as those gains are shared by all
4. Catching joy from successful efforts of each involved in a group effort
5. Increasing joy from the size of the group involved in creating a successful effort
6. Multiplying joy further within families involved, fed by the group in successful efforts

As previously mentioned in coping with the mental/emotional environment, it will take a courageous, brave effort by each individual. Depending on the personality of each person involved, the challenge may be more difficult for those who rely strongly on pleasing all the people around them. For them, it will mean that they will need to withstand trials on changing their associations to relationships that will further their direction toward freedom. It will also mean withstanding trials on changes in the use of their personal resources to move them in a stronger direction to freedom. Whether an outgoing or introverted personality, it will mean gaining new connections with others who are willing to work toward more individual freedom and less government dependence. It will mean coordinating and cooperating with others to make the changes needed in the way the country works. With the joint effort of other like-minded people, you will be able to celebrate achievement and be rewarded by progress toward a free and happy country.

"What more felicity can fall to creature,
Than to enjoy delight with liberty."

Sir Edmund Spenser (1552–1599),
writer and poet from "The Fate of the
Butterflie" (1591)

The joint efforts of people seeking lives that are nothing less than the freedom and opportunity for happiness that is a natural birthright will be a satisfying activity. It will help those involved feel good, feel happy, and bring about the rewards of freedom for all within a country.

GAINING A FREE AND HAPPY LIFE

WHERE WE CAME FROM

It is hard for those U.S. citizens who have lived there for the last fifty years to accept the current environment changes of a country with past high standards, high expectations, high employment, and high international respect. It is even harder for citizens who are now entering the work-force to visualize such an environment amid the declining standards, lower expectations, higher unemployment, and declining international respect.

Of the people inhabiting the United States, there are a small number of natives to the country. Many of the people who helped found and develop the country came from European countries where the government was composed of royalty in the form of kings and queens. Individuals had little say in their government and in their choice of religion. The societies, the cities, and the way people earned their living had developed over many centuries. Although the general environment was familiar from generations of adapting to their surroundings and the government that ruled them, there were some who felt that they could do better. When the citizens of the European countries found out that there was a country with land available an ocean away, some saw it as an opportunity for a new and different life. Over the next three centuries, the American continent was the destination of many who were responsible for the formation of the foundation of the United States.

The founding members of the United States had to have special qualities to leave countries, towns, societies, and ways of life they knew and to survive the unknowns of totally different environments of a new land. It should be obvious that they were risk takers. They had to be brave to face a different environment composed of these obstacles:

1. Minimal and still developing towns
2. Fearful, untrusting, and sometimes hostile natives
3. Start of new means of earning a living
4. General survival
5. Distance from the people and area they knew in the old country

In addition to the courage needed to leave their own country for a new, unknown country, the founding citizens of America were seekers of freedom. The founding citizens sought the following:

1. Freedom from the military and government dictates of government
2. Freedom to choose their religion
3. Free markets uncontrolled by government
4. More liberal legal restrictions

Although, in the early years of America, there was a strong influence of the government (English in the thirteen colonies, French in Canada and Louisiana, and Spanish in the Southwest), the vastness of the new land left much freedom to the settlers. Much of the influence of the governments was involved in the trade of goods and in collecting taxes. The early settlers grew less dependent on government and more independent.

The founding ancestors of the United States came to the new country as brave, courageous freedom seekers. They became strong, independent, confident, and responsible people for having survived and adapted to a new land. They developed a raw, undeveloped land; developed businesses and livings from nothing; developed local governments and services; and overcame the challenges of Native Americans. Using the confidence and self-reliance that the early settlers developed, they used the courage that brought them to America to fight for freedom and independence from England. When the founding ancestors formed their own national government, they wanted it to have all the positive traits that they felt were most desirable. They kept the most desirable qualities of the governments from their old lands. They also made it clear that their government would strengthen all the desirable qualities that they had developed in their experience. The government that the founders developed had these qualities:

1. Fairness across jurisdictional boundaries between states and between national and state governments
2. An established legal system to protect law-abiding citizens and punish those who were not
3. An insured domestic tranquility with rights of individuals to live in peace in their own manner and of their own choice
4. A common defense of citizens from those seeking to harm others
5. Promotion of the welfare of all citizens equally through the services of government without providing for any limited groups of citizens
6. Security of the blessings of life, liberty, and property that the founders felt were endowed as a birthright

The qualities that the founders wanted were basically to experience the freedom to enjoy life in a fair and orderly environment. After their experience with a national government that they felt was overbearing and restrictive, they were careful not to give too much power to the central government of their nation. Consequently, after the national government was formed, there was minimal government authority over the states and the citizens, as well as minimal taxation to pay for its activities.

WHERE WE ARE NOW

As mentioned in previous sections of this text, the authority of the central or federal government has expanded tremendously due, in great part, to the growth in power and independence of the Federal Reserve. This has happened because of the weak leadership of Congress as they found it easier to relinquish power over the economy to the Federal Reserve in trade for the ability to fund spending with printed money. Since 1971, without any tangible asset (gold) needed to support the value of the dollar, the Federal Reserve can manufacture (print) as many dollars as it takes to fund federal government operation. The citizens and taxpayers must watch as either their pay buys less (due to inflation) or their standard of living decreases as rising taxes leave less take-home pay available to purchase needed resources. As this text is written, Congress argues over how much to tax its citizens to pay for spending levels that even now far exceed the government's ability to pay for its operation. In the next few years, U.S. citizens will face higher taxes, more expensive federal government programs, and, at the same time, reduced standards of living. For those who are working, that will be the case. For those who are unable to find work, the case is much worse.

"You can't give the government the power to do good without also giving it the power to do bad—in fact, to do anything it wants. It is not so much the abuse of power which is a concern. It is the power to abuse."

Harry Browne, writer and politician (June 17, 1933–March 1, 2006)

There is a lack of confidence in Congress and the federal government, and it is much deserved. Citizens, those who vote, are coerced with more government benefits to elect members of Congress on the basis of so-called improvements, while they will then be expected to pay for them. Those benefits seem justified until they must be paid for. The cost is not only individual taxes, but taxes on the businesses that hire people and must make payroll. The lack of control by Congress over the federal budget has passed expenses down to states and cities to avoid openly and directly increasing taxes at the federal level. This tactic causes increased taxes and expenses at the state, local, and business levels. In addition to creating expensive benefits to buy votes, Congress has created special laws and regulations benefiting small groups in order to buy more votes. Without consideration of costs, it seems to citizens that this is just more benefits. Nevertheless, taxpayers must pay for the cost of helping benefit small groups in cases that would normally be applicable to general criminal or civil laws. This has all been the result of an irresponsible Congress that gained power through failure to control the Federal Reserve and the federal budget. The taxpaying U.S. citizen has been slowly turned into a dependent slave of the federal budget, depending on it for benefits and paying for benefits that help many more than contribute to its cost. The taxpaying U.S. citizen has been played for a fool by the Federal Reserve and Congress. The two political parties (Democratic and Republican) and the majority of the members of those parties are responsible for the current decline of the U.S. economy and standard of living.

Although it took almost forty years to reach the country's present weakened condition, we cannot allow the country to continue in the same direction. The United States is on the brink of an endless decline similar to England in the last century and to Japan at the beginning of this century. The country needs to set realistic goals to make the changes needed to insure that this generation and future generations will be able to attain the free and happy lives that are our birthright.

STRATEGIES TO GET TO A BETTER LIFE

ULTIMATE GOAL: ACHIEVING POTENTIAL FOR HAPPINESS

It is our birthright to gain the best use of our abilities. This can be done by using our freedom of choice to apply and develop our abilities over time and experience. Parents and authority figures have the responsibility to aid those under their care to help them gain use of their abilities and provide adequate freedom for developing into happy, satisfied people. Parents and related adults provide the early, most direct involvement in your growth and development. It is the responsibility of the various levels of government to influence the growth and development of you beyond parents and related contacts over your life. It was the wisdom of the founding members of the U.S. government that provided the Bill of Rights to guide the government in its responsibilities for the growth and development of each of us to achieve happy and productive lives. This is the overall goal that we, as parents and citizens of government, must provide.

"Come on now, all you young men, all over the world. You are needed more than ever now to fill the gap of a generation shorn by the war. You have not an hour to lose. You must take our places in life's fighting line. Twenty to twenty-five! These are the years! Don't be content with things as they are. The earth is yours and the fullness thereof.' Enter upon your inheritance,

accept your responsibilities. Raise the glorious flags again, advance them upon the new enemies, who constantly gather upon the front of the human army, and have only to be assaulted to be overthrown. Don't take no for an answer, never submit to failure. Do not be fobbed off with mere personal success or acceptance. You will make all kinds of mistakes; but as long as you are generous and true, and also fierce, you cannot hurt the world or even seriously distress her. She was made to be wooed and won by youth."

Winston Churchill (1874_1965), Prime Minister of England From While England Slept, 1936

The statement by Sir Winston Churchill was made prior to the Second World War. What the United States and the developed world face today is as important a crisis as the second big war of the last century. It is critical to the current generation and the next two generations, just as was the Second World War. The strategies that follow are as critical as any major battle in any war.

INSTALLING RESPONSIBLE LEADERSHIP

The country and its citizens reached the current negative environment with leaders who cared more for buying votes and satisfying their egos than the long-term welfare of the people they served. Both parties in Congress have allowed the gradual weakening of the country's citizens' independence; exploding the country's debt; encouraging citizens to increase their debt; dismantling the country's industry and the jobs they provide; and building a costly, restrictive bureaucracy. Without leadership that assigns priorities with consideration of logical, realistic budgets, the average citizen will get less net income and have less opportunity to improve his or her life. The two major political parties have been responsible for increased dependence on the national government, growth in the federal/national debt, and decreased freedom and the opportunity for happiness.

The leadership and direction of the United States need the best qualities of both the major parties instead of the worst. The freedom and happiness philosophy allows taking the best qualities of both parties. A party that closely follows the freedom philosophy view of the operation of government has been the Libertarian Party. The Libertarian Party is centered on the individual and using government to provide and support freedom so that individuals can reach their potential. It is the one party that closely resembles what the founding members of the U.S. government intended for the country's citizens. To learn about the party, you can look into www.lp.org at the issues and positions section. Although you may not agree with each of the positions there, when compared to the two major parties, there may be more agreement with what is needed. In order for you to choose the best leadership for your country, all three of the major parties must be considered. The Democratic Party's views on issues can be found at www.democrats.org, and the Republican Party's views on issues can be found at www.gop.com.

Because the U.S. Congress is where power and authority has become centered and has done the most harm to the country, the choices citizens make there can have the most impact on the country's future.

You can evaluate potential congressional representatives and senators on the following issues:

1. **Taxes**

   a. Taxes are necessary for paying the cost of government. The cost of government must be minimized. The two main functions of government that are required are: (a.) to protect citizens' individual constitutional rights (Bill of Rights) and (b.) to protect citizens from foreign attacks (harm).

   b. The function of transferring income from taxpaying individuals to bail out or subsidize nonproductive individuals, companies, and organizations restricts the freedom of taxpaying individuals to provide artificial support of qualities that detract from the general welfare of all citizens.

   c. Functions of government beyond protecting constitutional rights and protecting against foreign attacks (harm) should be privatized or made the responsibility of individuals.

2. **The economy: allow and support the free market**

   a. **Bailouts and subsidies:** transfer money from poor taxpayers to rich taxpayers and aids continued bad management. (Think AIG, giant banks, auto manufacturers, Fannie Mae, and Freddie Mac, while letting many local and regional banks fail.) There should be no bailouts or subsidies where a free market option is available.

   b. **Fiscal responsibility:** deficit spending eliminated to reduce the burden on present and future taxpayers. Privatize government services where possible.

   c. **Money supply and interest rates** should be managed by the Treasury with the Federal Reserve eliminated and interest rates set by the market for financing. Institute a gold-backed (valued resource) currency as before 1971 to provide a realistic value to money.

d. Energy policy

    i.   Allow individuals and businesses to make decisions on energy that are in line with a free and open market. Keep the federal/national government involved only to support the free market.

    ii.   Limit energy decisions to regulation by local and state governments that reflect the free choices and desires of the people most directly impacted within their jurisdiction.

    iii.   Allow and support the right of individuals to make their own free market decisions as to purchase and use of energy.

e. Business barrier elimination improves opportunities for business and job growth.

    i.   Remove the minimum wage requirement to allow payment for labor at a rate that allows all willing to work at the rate.

    ii.   Drop insurance requirements for employers and insurance companies to allow insuring individuals for what risks are most appropriate for the business and the individual.

    iii.   Eliminate government regulatory agencies to allow appropriate existing insurance requirements and legal liability requirements to minimize preventable risk of measurable damages to the public.

iv. Reform education to allow parents and students to choose to spend taxes at schools that provide the best education.

3. **Poverty and welfare**

   a. **War on poverty:** Forty years of attempts have been unsuccessful, except to increase dependence on government funds for individuals and groups. Food, housing, and income assistance from family and private support organizations (churches, charities, and foundations) must be increased to provide more effective and locally operated aid. Eliminate ineffective and inefficient government-operated welfare programs.

   b. **Aid tax credit:** Give taxpayers dollar-for-dollar credit against taxes for contribution to private support organizations. With less tax money filtered through government, there will be more funds available to private support organizations for more efficient and effective aid to individuals.

4. **Health care:** Safety and affordability must be gained through the free market.

   a. **Medical savings plans:** Allowing 100 percent tax-deductible savings for health needs that can carry a balance without penalty

   b. **Deregulated health insurance policies:** without mandated coverage so that only needed benefits are insured to avoid wasted funds

   c. **Eliminate regulatory agencies:** like the FDA who increases the cost and time to develop needed health care products. Using the free market of appropriate insurance requirements and legal liability requirements can minimize risk of measureable harm to the public.

d. **Private health care providers:** to minimize cost and maximize efficiency of providing care for individuals. This reduces the costs that taxpayers must fund to provide benefits for those who could pay for themselves.

5. Civil liberties

a. **Bill of Rights** limited the power of the federal or central government as it should be. Authority of the federal government must be reduced and more authority transferred to state and local governments—without transferring budget and expense responsibilities. Increase the role of state and local citizens in the decisions and regulations to which they are subjected.

b. **Right to privacy:** Each individual has the right to privacy in their personal information and property. With today's technology, there is no need to use Social Security Identification as a requirement for identification for law-abiding citizens.

c. **Freedom of speech and press:** Control and authority over communications should be limited only by liability for actual and measureable damages.

d. **Freedom to own guns** is the individuals' right to own a gun and have the right to defend themselves. Because criminals are likely to be armed, with more citizens armed there will be more risk for criminals in harming individual citizens and less crime.

e. **Tort laws and risk:** There must be a risk to starting a lawsuit. If an individual or group of individuals files an unsuccessful lawsuit, they should pay all legal costs involved in an unsuccessful verdict. This will reduce the cost of business, insurance, and medical care.

6. **Crime and violence**

   a. **Victim's rights:** Victims of crimes have the right to testify in the trial and punishment of an accused perpetrator as well as having the right to restitution by a convicted criminal.

   b. **Eliminate prohibition of victimless crimes:** Much time and money is spent on prosecuting adult individuals for making the free choice of what they will do with their own bodies. It is wasteful of taxpayers' money to prosecute and punish individuals for exercising the freedom of choice that does no harm to anyone else.

   c. **Fair and complete punishment:** When crimes are punished and the many victimless crimes do not fill prisons, there should be no early releases only to clear space in prisons. Restitution to the victims of crimes must be part of a complete punishment.

   d. **Right to defend:** There should be no punishment for a potential victim who uses a gun or other weapon to prevent a verified attack by a criminal.

   e. **Education:** The education process should include the importance of an independent existence and the Bill of Rights to promote freedom of the individual and the right to happiness.

7. **Military environment**

   a. **Iraq and Afghanistan:** Military involvement should happen only until relative order in government is established in the short-term. Economic involvement should happen only to establish capitalism, with trade only in the best interests of the citizens of the United States. All involvement necessary should be limited to the importance of establishing stable government in the Middle East.

b. **Middle East:** Withdraw all military involvement with the exception of support for temporary involvement in Iraq and Afghanistan. Give trade and economic support for those countries where it is in the best interest of maintaining energy supplies. If oil independence is established for the United States, the only involvement in the region will be trade for the benefit of U.S. citizens.

c. **Global military presence:** This should be concentrated only in the geographic locations where a military presence is needed to maintain supply of a rare and limited material that is required by citizens of the United States and cannot be obtained by trade. Reduction of present deployments, outside of the Middle East, should happen over several years. Bases should be turned over (sold) to allies or sold to private businesses.

d. **Defense of United States:** The ultimate and only goal of military involvement. The technology and weaponry developed for military use is to defend and protect U.S. citizens. Major budget reductions and less global presence produce lower expenses from foreign deployments.

8. **Environment**

a. **End sovereign immunity:** Levels of government own or control much of the natural environment. Government must be as responsible as anyone for damage to the environment, whether or not the asset is owned by the government.

b. **Restitution for damages:** Whether the government owns or controls an environmental asset or not, damages to the environment should be paid by the entity that causes the damage.

c. **Private ownership of environmental assets:** All environmental assets should be sold to realize the highest value and most effective use of those assets. This will reduce the government budget debt, while gaining the most efficient and effective use of those assets.

HOW TO JUDGE CANDIDATES ON THE ABOVE ISSUES

1. Make a list of the eight sections and subsections listed above and become familiar with each position and issue affecting them. Question the candidates for your congressional Representative and Senate offices on each of the above issues. As politicians, they will likely have position papers on each issue. Do not be surprised if they have positions on both sides of an issue.

2. Use the candidates' Web site or local appearances to tie them down on several views that seem to disagree with each other.

3. The potential candidates should meet at least 66 percent (two-thirds) positive agreement with the above issues to warrant supporting them for a position.

4. If not meeting the minimum level of agreement, support should be given to the Libertarian candidate to send a message to the two main parties that they are losing support. Of course, if there is one issue that most strongly affects you or your family, you should support what is best for yourself and your family.

5. When you have identified the candidate you feel is best for the position, use your time and resources to promote the candidate and his or her views. Use your time, funds, and contacts (Internet sites, social organizations, work contacts, etc.) to urge voting and voting for the chosen candidate.

State and local government officials are also important because they have the most direct impact and are most directly influenced by the citizens they serve. Career politicians are less likely at these levels because they must be more responsive to all the citizens they serve. They cannot accept a local benefit in return for obligations to help others outside of their district. Nevertheless, many of the local and state officials contest for congressional positions as they rise in the political arena. It is most important to identify candidates who place their citizens' long-term interests first. The same procedure can be used for state and local candidates as for congressional candidates. A quality that freedom-seeking individuals will want in a state or local candidate would be a strong belief in control of governmental services and benefits being administered by the smallest and lowest level of government. Although the pay may be lower and candidates less knowledgeable, the influence and local impact are closest to the citizens they serve. As this philosophy spreads, the strength and competence of state and local leaders will be the key to individuals, states, and the country attaining their maximum potential.

BALANCING THE FEDERAL BUDGET

One of the most important actions that responsible congressional representatives can do is to gain control of federal spending. They must also reduce the tax and regulatory burden that the central government has created. Budget control is more than a matter of reducing dollars spent and is focused on regaining the independence of individuals. Just as state and local governments have been able to operate with balanced budgets, so can the national government. Spending has to be financed with realistic revenue levels used to pay for federal government programs and not by "created" funds from printing money. In addition to taxes, the federal government has assets that can be sold to supplement spending and can contract with independent companies to perform many functions at lower costs. Just as many states and cities have done to balance their budgets, so can the national government.

Spending on subsidies for businesses, organizations, and countries that do not provide a reasonable and realistic return on the country's investment should be eliminated over four to six years, or a similarly reasonable time. Military involvement in countries nonessential to the safety and security of U.S. citizens should be eliminated in four to six years, or a similarly reasonable time.

The number and size of federal agencies should be reduced to create a more responsive, less expensive system to coordinate efforts at state and regional levels. The cost of federal agencies can be reduced while increasing the freedom and abilities of states and cities to best utilize their resources. The resources of independent businesses and companies can be used to regulate business operations and reduce risks. Where free market operations are allowed, risk to citizens can be reduced through risk of loss by service providers through legal and insurance actions against them.

The funding of laws and regulations that govern free choices of adult individuals must be eliminated to reduce the expenses of enforcing, trying, and imprisoning people for harming no one but themselves. This will reduce the power of organized crime and free time and funds to protect citizens' rights and freedoms from true criminal actions. Taxes on victimless crime activities can be used to reduce property and income taxes. Those taxes can support realistic state and local law enforcement to protect law-abiding citizens.

With real, responsible leaders in Congress, all budget items can be reduced instead of expanded as has been the case for the last forty years. It will take a stronger will to serve all citizens equally, but at reduced levels, to gain control of the federal budget. It will mean ending the use of the Federal Reserve expansion of money supply to inflate incomes to increase tax revenues. As control of taxes and spending is gained, it will also mean ending the loss of purchasing power and lower disposable income levels.

Gaining control of the federal budget will transfer responsibility for individual actions back to each citizen and away from the national government. Each citizen will be more independent and have the opportunity to focus time and resources on using his or her freedom to seek the best opportunities for happiness.

REORDERING THE LEVELS OF GOVERNMENT

The United States and similarly large countries have diverse local conditions of weather, soil, transportation systems, resources, and history that give each area distinct advantages. Policies, regulations, and laws that are made at the national level must apply to all states and localities, yet national policies, regulations, and laws do not allow each state and locality to sufficiently maximize its potential. If more authority is centered near the unique qualities of an area, it is much more likely for that area to reach its maximum potential to achieve the happiness of the citizens. With government authority close to and better coordinated with the unique qualities of an area, the creativity of that area can better utilize and maximize those qualities.

The current system of dominant national government in the U.S. works contrary to what will be best for states and localities. A strong national government gives unwarranted security from risks to "too big to fail businesses" because they feel that the national government will bail out their mistakes. All U.S. taxpayers will pay for bailing out housing in Michigan, Florida, California, and Nevada. They will also pay for bailing out AIG, CitiGroup, Bank of America, Goldman Sachs, General Motors, Chrysler, and other large businesses. If the national government and the Federal Reserve had been operated like state or local governments, the enormous deficit and wasted bailout funds may never have happened.

All authority cannot be moved to the state and local level, but coordination among states must be supported at the national level. The current economic crisis is the result of uncontrolled spending by and a greatly expanded role of the national government. The national budget must be balanced and include policies, regulations, and laws that give the states the most freedom in applying them to the local area. The "one size fits all" role of dominant national government must be reduced. More authority and the freedom to use it must be transferred to state and local governments. Reduced bureaucracy and budgets at the national level will then allow each state and local government to best use local resources. With local resources able to maximize their potential, the citizens in each area will have the best opportunity to use their freedom to gain happiness. If all state and local areas maximize their resources and develop their economies, the country will gain from the sum of the local successes. In short, the freedom of each locality to maximize their potential from their resources benefits the nation as a whole.

LIMITING AND ELIMINATING THE FEDERAL RESERVE

Since 1971, the Federal Reserve has been responsible for the growth in the authority of the U.S. central government, the growth in the national budget deficit, the surge in the stock and housing bubbles, and the growth in the power of the Federal Reserve in international banking and finance. With the tremendous growth of the U.S. economy and financial presence, the global economy became strongly dependent upon consumers in the United States. Even the depressed economy in Japan since 1989 did not stop the growth in the U.S. economy. The consumer growth in the United States was fueled by strong and steady money supply growth from the Federal Reserve. Many of the developed nations in the Americas and Europe followed the example of the Federal Reserve in excessive money supply growth. The beneficiaries of the strong consumer growth of the developed countries were the low wage countries of Asia and South America. When the U.S. economy began its collapse in 2007, the economies of the developed countries that had followed the Federal Reserve's lead all collapsed with it.

The "cure" that the Federal Reserve and the central banks that follow its lead has been to flood the vaults of large financial institutes with money. In the United States, that means dollars that are printed pieces of paper. Because the large financial institutes lost much of their assets in gambles in the financial derivative markets, little of the money has reached the creators of jobs and growth in the economy. The creators of jobs and economic growth have been small and medium-sized businesses in the history of the United States. Unfortunately, because the Federal Reserve caused bubbles in the stock market, housing, and consumer goods from its management of the money supply, it will take years for the U.S. economy to recover. Recovery will only happen when the United States can regain some of the income from production of goods that was lost to the low-wage countries of Asia and Latin America. That will mean that the low-wage countries must increase their income enough to buy developed countries' expensive products. The developed countries must reduce their income to make their wages more competitive in the production of goods. In short, the developed countries' competitors for work must increase their standard of living while the developed countries reduce their standard of living.

The way to avoid future ups and downs in the U.S. economy will be for the money supply to be managed to benefit all citizens and not to benefit large financial institutions. This cannot be done with an operation that is run for and by the large financial institutions and not for and by U.S. citizens. As imperfect as representative government is, it will be better for the national money supply to be managed by the Treasury and overseen by Congress and the president. Although past presidents have been given credit for the performance of the economy, the Federal Reserve has been the major player in the management of the money supply. With the money supply managed in the interest of the citizens and not in the interest of large financial institutions, there will be no one to blame for the direction of the economy by people who represent the citizens. There will be no one to blame for major economic crises but ourselves.

The Federal Reserve was able to gain dominance when the world no longer had any means of measuring the true value of the dollar. After 1971, the dollar became a piece of paper that supposedly had a value, but strangely enough it took larger and larger quantities to buy real assets. There must be some real basis to measure the buying power of the currency used for exchange for goods and services. If not, over time, each person will find that the same amount of work buys less and less. Examples can be seen by looking around and seeing how many average households now require at least two adults working to supply basic food, clothing, transportation, and housing. The current enormous increase in the money supply and enormous increase in the budget deficit guarantee that there will be increases in inflation in the future. Inflation will not be cured by using gold or another stable resource to measure a currency's value. The currency value will, however, be a free market based measure instead of a number manipulated to provide the best political measure.

With dependable members of Congress, it will be possible to change the responsibility of the Treasury to managing money supply and remove the authority from the Federal Reserve. Congress formed the Federal Reserve in 1913 and can change how money supply is handled in the future. Until that change is made, the Federal Reserve must be open to audit as to how it works, as is any company in the country. It will also be possible to reinstate the gold standard to keep a realistic basis on management of the money supply and its value.

Gaining control of the money supply and the general direction of the economy will clear up who is responsible for the direction of the economy. Today, depending upon reporting by various media sources, the president, the Congress, the Secretary of the Treasury, the Federal Reserve chairman, or big business capitalists are either blamed or credited for the direction of the economy. The economy is much too complex for any one person or group to control. More clarity in the responsibility for its direction can be gained by centering the money supply and financing of the country's budget in the Treasury under the direction of the president and Congress. With representatives of the citizens that support the free market and responsible control of the federal budget, we will have a better chance of gaining happiness in our lives.

RESTORING A CONSTITUTIONAL COURT

In the last fifty years, Supreme Court decisions have attempted to give clearer interpretations of the Bill of Rights. Those interpretations have, for the most part, broadened the original intent of the Constitution to assure equal rights to all citizens and property owners. The result of these efforts has been to complicate laws and regulations to cause enforcement to become more difficult and time-consuming. No doubt there was a need to remove such freedom-robbing practices as slavery, but the broad interpretation of "rights" has morphed into rights specific to groups (race, sexual orientation, ability, language, income, housing, appearance, employment, etc.). Congress and state legislatures have attempted to solve questions and issues of rights by adding interpretations to aid particular constituencies in their voting districts. As issues developed with those laws and regulations, courts at the state and national levels have been called upon to determine what they considered to be just.

Unfortunately for the United States, the growing power of the Federal Reserve evolved into a Congress solving problems without regard to cost. It became easier to buy votes with laws and regulations. There was no regard to cost by Congress because, since 1971, the Federal Reserve could print money to make up for deficit spending. The ability to solve problems and address issues without concern for spending controls made U.S. residents more dependent on the national government. With Congress leading the nation to dependence on them for solving all problems, the broad interpretation of citizens' rights grew. Congressional and presidential appointments to the Supreme Court followed the general thinking of a need for the broadest interpretation of laws and regulations.

The courts take far longer to change direction because judges' terms are long or unlimited. With new, responsible congressional and legislative leaders in government, the influence they have on laws, regulations, and court positions can change. Initially, the change can be in the laws and regulations themselves, but over time, the change will happen with who and how court members are approved. The current situation did not happen overnight as the change in the direction of people's thinking was gradual. Judges are public servants and attempt to serve in the best interests of the public. Changes in public thinking will bring about more independent, responsible citizens. Those citizens will elect more responsible leaders. The decisions of sitting judges should then follow suit in doing what is best for the public.

The changes to the court system will be slow. The changes will be in the direction of allowing individuals, businesses, and government freedom to make decisions in the best interest of all and with equal rights to all.

GOALS OF A BETTER LIFE

GENERAL

As previously stated, the ultimate goal is for achieving your maximum potential for happiness. The responsibility for helping to achieve that goal starts with parents and close relationships and, in time, transfers to you and the government under which you live. The world is complex. The environment that you experience is complex. Your mind is complex. The relationships that you experience are complex. There is no guarantee of freedom or happiness. God, or whatever one chooses to believe, gives us life and gives you the desire for freedom. All seek freedom and what they perceive to be freedom. As you gain your share of freedom, it is up to you to use that freedom to increase happiness in your life. Seeking and gaining freedom and increasing the happiness in your life are up to you. Joy and happiness can be increased and multiplied by aiding or sharing happiness with others for a better life.

GOAL FOR INDIVIDUALS

Reward is in proportion to risk. Rewards work both positively and negatively. Without risk, there will not be any great harm, but there cannot be greater reward. Joy and happiness can only be achieved with actions that result in outcomes that exceed the expected. Risk has been reduced by the central government at great expense to individual taxpayers and businesses. Risk reduction has reduced satisfaction and personal achievement while increasing dependence. The opportunity for happiness can only be attained with you gaining independence and assuming personal responsibility by allowing risks in your life. Applying the philosophy of freedom and happiness will result in you becoming more independent and responsible. You will thus achieve a greater opportunity for happiness than has been seen for fifty years.

GOAL FOR GOVERNMENT

Government will change its deficit spending, risk reduction, and income transfer activity to allow major reductions in central government requirements. The major changes in central government operation will greatly reduce budget requirements. Greatly reduced budget requirements will allow equal and reduced tax levels to taxpayers. A great reduction in central government will thus reduce the tax burden and impact on the daily life of individuals and businesses. This will give the individual taxpayer more disposable income and more opportunity for jobs as businesses have greater funds to invest in growing their business and the jobs they provide. More disposable income for you will allow you the opportunity to purchase more goods. With more retail activity and less tax liability, businesses will be able to price more competitively and can compete with lower cost foreign suppliers. Applying freedom and happiness to government will change it to a supporter of economic activity instead of an obstacle to overcome.

GOAL FOR BUSINESS

Business will act in partnership with the government to grow revenues, profits, and jobs. Decisions will be made on the basis of return on investment. Consideration of stable, logical regulations will evolve to improving growth and competitiveness. The free market will decide costs of materials and labor for producing goods. Taxes and regulations will be minimized within the country. It will encourage growth and competitiveness in free, fair, and equal markets. Regulations will be based on fair and equal treatment for all. A stable, supportive regulatory environment will encourage growth and jobs. Although labor costs can-

not compete with foreign labor and benefits, tax allowances for technological and capital investment will support U.S. industries' competitiveness. No subsidies, outside of technology and capital tax reductions,
are given to businesses. By gaining control of the federal budget, the
taxes on businesses can be set at a single low rate. The capital gains tax
on stocks can be eliminated to provide improved ability for financing
for businesses. The businesses in the United States will operate in a free
market, with limited requirements for benefits, regulations, and taxes to
create more growth and jobs. That growth of business and jobs will give
you the best opportunity for happiness in the future.

GOAL FOR THE LEGAL SYSTEM

The legal system will function in a more simple and economical atmosphere. The waste of time and funds in regulating victimless crimes
will free funds to concentrate on preventing criminal actions that harm
individuals and businesses. Individuals will be held accountable for
causing measureable harm to others and will pay realistic, actual damages to those harmed. Criminal offences will be fully punished and
victims fully compensated. Risk of full punishment for criminal actions
reduces their occurrence. Civil lawsuits will be minimized as risk of
filing poorly supported actions reduces them. Reduction in the possibility of unfounded civil lawsuits reduces insurance and operating costs.
Improvement in the economics of law enforcement provides better protection for businesses and individuals. Businesses and you will be free
to operate and live in a safe environment to have your best chance for
happiness.

GOAL FOR RELIGION

No matter what belief you have, you must have the opportunity to gain
happiness without harm. No religion or belief can claim to be good, if

its followers believe that they have the right to harm another. You must have the freedom to choose what you believe and how you practice those beliefs. Government will have the right to acknowledge God, but should not require anyone to believe in any particular religion. You have the right to believe or not believe in God or any particular religion. Religion is one area where freedom must be allowed. Whether you believe in God or any religion, you should follow guidelines in your life to avoid harm and/or provide help to others where needed. We must have the freedom to choose to be good so that we can gain happiness for ourselves and for others.

CLOSING GOAL

The purpose of writing this book was to show how a philosophy that can be accepted by all could make the world a better place. Applying the philosophy is a process that promotes freedom of the individual, so that you can gain happiness. Although this process is for the individual, attaining the goals listed above requires working with others. To put this in perspective, the best chance for your freedom means working in cooperation with others to reach the necessary goals. Beyond only working with others, it also means using those relationships to achieve specific ends or goals. Those relationships must also be used to successfully implement actions and interpret media messages to make the right choices. All the goals above are important as end results, but the strategies and the improvements provide the road to gaining those goals. With success in implementing the improvements and the strategies provided, the ultimate goal of achieving your maximum potential for happiness can be realized.

Our Freedom

When God made me
he made me to be free.
He gave me a life
with both joy and strife.

The choices are all mine
to darken or make shine.
With the energy that I give
to the way that I live.

I will cause no alarm
and do no one any harm.
I must be allowed to be free
and live a life that is me.

Made in the USA
Charleston, SC
24 December 2011